"Geisler and Tunnicliffe have hit a grand slam with this little book. For compressing so many vital Christian truths into so few pages, I'm not sure this book has a rival. I heartily recommend it to all young people who have started to doubt their Christian faith. Better yet, read this book before such doubts appear—it provides an incredible amount of ammunition to deal with the assaults on faith that our culture and educational system constantly throw at us. Here is Christian apologetics at its best!"

—William A. Dembski, Senior Fellow, Discovery Institute, author of *The Design Inference*

"*Reasons for Belief* is vintage Geisler—crisp, correct, concise, and courageous. Written for the Christian who needs answers, not encyclopedias."

—Paige Patterson, Southwestern Baptist Theological Seminary, Fort Worth, Texas

Books by Norman L. Geisler

FROM BETHANY HOUSE PUBLISHERS

If God, Why Evil?   *Unshakable Foundations*

Chosen But Free   *Reasons for Belief*

Systematic Theology

FROM BAKER PUBLISHING GROUP

Christian Ethics, rev. ed.   *Matters of Life and Death*

The Apologetics of Jesus   *Come Let Us Reason*

Making Sense of Bible   *Apologetics in the New Age*
Difficulties
                                       Introduction to Philosophy
The Big Book of Bible
Difficulties   *Worlds Apart*

Where Skeptics Ask   *Christian Apologetics*

A Popular Survey of the Old   *Origin Science*
Testament
                                       Is Man the Measure?
Why I Am a Christian
                                       What Augustine Says
Correcting the Cults
                                       The Creator in the Courtroom:
Answering Islam, rev. ed.   *Scopes II*

Baker Encyclopedia of   *Options in Contemporary*
Christian Apologetics   *Christian Ethics*

Roman Catholics and   *To Understand the Bible,*
Evangelicals   *Look for Jesus*

Miracles and the Modern Mind

REASONS FOR BELIEF

Easy-to-Understand Answers to 10 Essential Questions

NORMAN L. GEISLER
AND PATTY TUNNICLIFFE

BETHANY HOUSE PUBLISHERS
a division of Baker Publishing Group
Minneapolis, Minnesota

© 2013 by Norman L. Geisler and Patty Tunnicliffe

Published by Bethany House Publishers
11400 Hampshire Avenue South
Bloomington, Minnesota 55438
www.bethanyhouse.com

Bethany House Publishers is a division of
Baker Publishing Group, Grand Rapids, Michigan

Printed in the United States of America

Library of Congress Cataloging-in-Publication Data
Geisler, Norman L.
    Reasons for belief : easy-to-understand answers to 10 essentialquestions / Norman L. Geisler and Patty Tunnicliffe.
        p.   cm.
    Includes bibliographical references.
    Summary: "A concise step-by-step study of the foundations of Christian faith in easy-to-understand language"—Provided by publisher.
    ISBN 978-0-7642-1057-0 (pbk. : alk. paper)
    1. Christianity—Miscellanea. 2. Apologetics—Miscellanea. I. Tunnicliffe, Patty. II. Title.
    BR121.3.G45 2013   2012
    239—dc23   2012039401

Cover design by Gearbox

13 14 15 16 17 18 19   7 6 5 4 3 2 1

Contents

Contents

1

A Basic Question in Need of an Answer

"Why Are You a Christian?"

Has anyone ever asked you this? It's a fair question, and also a pretty simple one. The inquirer wants to know why you believe in Jesus rather than in someone or something else.

It's like being asked why you're a fan of a certain team. Maybe you like the quarterback or one of the other players. Maybe you're loyal to your area or hometown or school. Maybe you're related to the coach. Whatever your reasons, you do have them for why you support and root for that team, and you'd gladly, probably even proudly, list them if someone wanted to know.

In the same way, if someone wants to know why you're a Christian, they want to know why you have chosen to follow Jesus instead of Muhammad or Buddha or somebody else.

Why are you a believer instead of an atheist or an agnostic? What are your reasons for being a Christian?

Whether or not you've yet been asked, sooner or later this question will come up. People are curious about religion, and many talk openly about their own ideas. Many celebrities promote some form of Buddhism. Tom Cruise and John Travolta are well-known to be Scientologists. Madonna has advocated her Kabbalist beliefs; Demi Moore, Paris Hilton, Ashton Kutcher, and others have dabbled with or delved into Kabbalah. Various organizations promote seminars designed to develop the different aspects of "spirituality." There are lots of other examples in almost as many different directions.

If you *have* been asked why you are a Christian, what was your answer? Do you think your response made sense to the person who asked it? Did it seem to satisfy their curiosity? Were you comfortable with what you said?

Many struggle with this, often feeling they can't come up with a straightforward, concise response. "Because Christianity is true" or "Because I believe the Bible" or "Because I love Jesus" (for example) might not be helpful or even make sense to the person asking.

Suppose you had only a moment to answer. How would you reply? Every believer should be, and can be, prepared with a response.

Our Culture Itself Is a Challenge

Not too long ago, most Americans accepted the basic claims of Christianity, even if they weren't Christians. Most believed there is a God. Most respected the Bible. Most were convinced

Jesus was an actual historical person. And most generally accepted the biblical moral code: Don't use God's name as a curse word; respect your parents; don't commit murder, lie, steal, or covet your neighbor's spouse or possessions.

This is no longer true. Many reject Christianity's core principles. Virtually everything Christians have always believed is being challenged or opposed. These challenges come from schoolteachers, college professors, commentators, writers—seemingly from every walk of life.

These are some of the allegations:

- There is no God.

- The New Testament is unreliable. Though it may have some good moral teaching, it contains fables and errors.

- If Jesus existed at all, he was not God; he certainly did not rise from the dead.

- The Bible is no different from any other religious book. All religions have their own truth.

- Many paths lead to God; Jesus is not the only way. Being good and being sincere about what you believe is what matters.

Many Christians don't know how to respond to these claims. They may believe they've found the truth but can't explain why it's true or why contrasting or contradictory beliefs are false. So they keep quiet. They love God, yet they hope no one asks "Why are you a Christian?"

Why Is This Important?

Today people from all over the world are living in the United States. Many know little about Christianity. Some have never considered the evidence for faith in Christ. Some have sincere and substantial questions about the Bible, God, or Jesus. Some only know what they see on TV or read online. Many young people only know what they hear from their parents, friends, or teachers.

People are right to ask questions about Christianity. They're right to ask how we can know that it's true; it's unreasonable to believe something unless there's evidence that it's correct. Anyone searching for God will want to find believable evidence that he exists. Anyone thinking of committing their life to anything will want to know why they should do so. What's the evidence that Jesus is God or that he died to forgive our sins?

Evidence does not save us, but many have turned to God when presented with the facts. God can and will use evidence to bring people to a saving knowledge of Jesus Christ. The apostle Paul offered evidence for the faith when he "reasoned" with people about its foundational claims (Acts 17:16–34). Many who heard him "were persuaded" (Acts 17:4) and became believers.

Everyone who's ever become a Christian had some reason to believe that doing so made sense. For example, they believed that there is a God, that Jesus is God, and that he died on the cross for their sins.

The Bible encourages everyone to seek God. It promises:

If you seek him, he will be found by you. (1 Chronicles 28:9)

You will seek me and find me when you seek me with all your heart. (Jeremiah 29:13)

Christianity provides honest answers backed up by evidence for the questions people ask. We need to know how to respond, though. We need to prepare ourselves to provide a biblical answer to life's biggest questions.

God has provided the current generation with more verification for the truth than at any previous time. Evidence substantiating the truth of the Bible has expanded rapidly in the past century. More than in any other era, we have access to powerful evidence for the God of the Bible, for the reliability of the Old and New Testaments, and for the deity and resurrection of Jesus.

The fact that God has sovereignly provided all this, now, is no accident. He expects us to know it and use it, and this isn't optional—the Bible directs us to be ready to defend our faith, so we're to be able to use facts and good reasoning to support what we believe.

Always be prepared to give an answer to everyone who asks you to give the reason for the hope that you have . . . with gentleness and respect. (1 Peter 3:15)

The question is, can we do this? Are we equipped and ready to respond when someone asks, "Why are you a Christian?"

Ten Challenges to Christianity

Here are ten primary challenges facing believers today. We'll address each one. Every chapter that follows will help equip you to better explain the truth and explain why you believe.

> ### Key Term: Apologetics
>
> *Apologetics* doesn't mean to say you're sorry for something but rather to defend something, to give reasons that support what you believe is true. Apologetics is what we're doing through this book; its goal is to assist you in becoming a strong defender of your faith.

Challenge #1: "Real truth does not exist. 'Truth' is just truth to you." (See chapter 2.)

Challenge #2: "God does not exist." (See chapters 3–4.)

Challenge #3: "If God exists, he isn't necessarily the God of the Bible." (See chapter 5.)

Challenge #4: "Miracles don't happen." (See chapter 6.)

Challenge #5: "The New Testament's many errors make it unreliable. It's more like a collection of myths and legends." (See chapter 7.)

Challenge #6: "Jesus never claimed to be God." (See chapter 8.)

Challenge #7: "Jesus didn't prove he is God." (See chapter 9.)

Challenge #8: "Jesus did not rise from the dead." (See chapter 10.)

Challenge #9: "The Bible isn't the only true religious book." (See chapter 11.)

Challenge #10: "Christianity is too narrow. There are many ways to God besides Jesus." (See chapter 12.)

How We'll Respond to These Challenges

We'll approach this as a defense attorney would when seeking to prove a defendant innocent of a charge. They'd present solid evidence. They'd establish a fact-based alibi. To prove innocence beyond a reasonable doubt, they might appeal to fibers, prints, marks or tracks, even DNA.

We'll look at many facts. We'll examine eyewitness accounts. We'll appeal to science, to history and archaeology, and to prophecy. We'll appeal to manuscript evidence and more.

See the chart below for the steps we'll take as we build our case.

**Ten Points That Answer Our Ten Challenges
and Prove Christianity Is True**

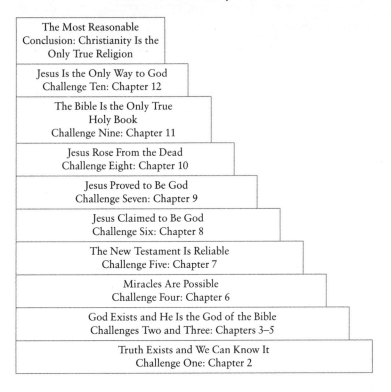

The Most Reasonable
Conclusion: Christianity Is the
Only True Religion

Jesus Is the Only Way to God
Challenge Ten: Chapter 12

The Bible Is the Only True
Holy Book
Challenge Nine: Chapter 11

Jesus Rose From the Dead
Challenge Eight: Chapter 10

Jesus Proved to Be God
Challenge Seven: Chapter 9

Jesus Claimed to Be God
Challenge Six: Chapter 8

The New Testament Is Reliable
Challenge Five: Chapter 7

Miracles Are Possible
Challenge Four: Chapter 6

God Exists and He Is the God of the Bible
Challenges Two and Three: Chapters 3–5

Truth Exists and We Can Know It
Challenge One: Chapter 2

Learning the facts isn't the ultimate end. Whatever proves to be true should impact our whole lives. So if you already believe, as you go through this book, pray that the information will help you to love God at a deeper level than you have before. Pray that it will help you to love him more with all your heart, soul, mind, and strength. And pray for opportunities to share the truth of God's Word with others.

Each chapter will define terms and explain ideas with the intent of making them basic and straightforward. If a word or concept isn't clear at first, be patient. If you feel stuck at any point, you could ask someone for an explanation or illustration, or you might look up something unfamiliar in an online dictionary.

Let's start with our first challenge, a challenge about truth.

2

Truth

Challenge #1: "Real Truth Does Not Exist.
'Truth' Is Just Truth to You"

Potential problem: Most people probably would agree that truth is important, since no one wants to believe something that isn't true. However, people also have very different ideas about what's true. Christianity claims to be the Truth, and thus claims that whatever contradicts it—every other religion—is false. Many today contend that "truth" is only true to the person who believes it. These assertions can't both be correct.

Teachers will say that two plus two *does* equal four. They'll tell you George Washington *was* the first U.S. president. They'll say there *is* a physical law we call the *law of gravity*. Statements like these are called *truth claims.*

Each day we all make statements we want others to accept as fact. That is, we make truth claims. Whenever someone asks where you live, or when your birthday is, your response is a truth claim, and you expect others to believe that what you've said is true. They expect the same of you when they make similar statements. Every day life is filled with truth claims.

Two Contradictory Views: What Is Meant by "Truth"

Since life is permeated with truth claims, there's no avoiding them, so we need to address this issue right away. Generally, there are two ideas about truth today.

View #1: Truth Is What's True for You

In this view, truth is relative—a subjective opinion. "Truth" becomes true to you as you believe it. In other words, *I'm convinced of it, so that settles it.* Someone with this view might say, "You have your truth, and I have mine."

View #2: Truth Is What Matches the Facts

In this view, truth is absolute—an objective reality. Truth isn't personal, and it doesn't belong to me or to you. Whether everyone, or most, or few, or nobody believes it, truth is what matches up with what's real. In other words, *It's true, so that settles it, whether or not I believe it.*

So What *Is* Truth?

Here is a solid definition: "*Truth* is what matches reality." Or again, "Truth matches the facts." People once believed the earth was flat and thought that if you sailed too far from land you'd fall off. It is true that people believed this, but that didn't make it true. The earth was and is round, no matter what anyone has believed. No opinion about the planet's shape has altered reality.

Another way to describe truth is to say, "Truth is telling it like it is." What we claim to be true must match the way things really are. My claim to have a thousand dollars in my savings account is only true if I actually have a thousand dollars there. If only a hundred dollars is in my account, my statement isn't true—I did not tell it like it is.

Conversely, something is a *falsehood* if it does not match reality, if it does not tell it like it is. While insistence that Santa Claus really exists and has flying reindeer, including one with a red nose, might serve make-believe fun for kids, it isn't actually true. It's false because it does not match reality.

How Can We *Know* What Is True?

We have said that truth must match the real world—the way things really are. It must "tell it like it is." So how can we know? Two tests can help us discover whether or not something is true.

Test #1: Examining All the Facts to See What Matches Reality

Truth must be backed up by facts, supported by outside evidence rather than personal opinions. Here are three examples of what some people believe despite the facts: The Holocaust never happened (the Nazis didn't murder millions of Jews); the U.S. never landed anyone on the moon (it was a faked performance); a group of Jews attacked the World Trade Center.

17

How would you show that these statements are untrue? You could use WWII newsreels, for example, to substantiate the Holocaust. You could appeal to the eyewitness testimony of those who worked on the lunar landing and of those who actually went. You could point to all of the evidence left behind by those who hijacked the planes on 9/11. Basically: You could prove your case by collecting the facts.

Some Truths About Truth

1. We don't invent truth; we discover it. In the early 1500s, Ferdinand Magellan sailed around the world by heading west and returning from the east. His demonstration of the earth's roundness wasn't the invention of a new truth. Rather, he discovered what had always been true.

2. Our understanding of the truth can change, but truth itself does not change. After Magellan's voyage, people had a new understanding of what had always been true: The earth is round.

3. Truth does not depend on how fervently or sincerely we believe something to be true. The correct answer to this true/false question: "The Twin Towers in New York City were attacked on September 11, 2000" is false. The date was September 11, 2001. It wouldn't matter how strongly someone believed that event took place in 2000; the answer is still false.

4. When something is true, it's true everywhere, for all people, at all times. Some cultures used to believe a dragon living under the earth (not the movement of tectonic plates) caused earthquakes—that the earth moved when the dragon moved. It's true that they believed this, but that didn't make it true. No one's beliefs make anything true or false. Truth is true, and falsehood is false, no matter what anyone believes.

Test #2: Learning to Think Correctly (Logically)

God has instituted certain unbreakable laws that operate throughout the universe. These are found, for instance, throughout the sciences, math, and even music. Two plus two is always four; if this varied from time to time or place to place, we couldn't operate machinery or computers—we couldn't even build a house. Middle C always vibrates at a certain frequency. If this varied from place to place, musicians couldn't tune their instruments accurately. There are even unbreakable laws regarding color. If you mix red and yellow, you'll always get orange, or some shade of orange—you'll never get green.

If we could break these laws, or if they only worked some of the time, the entire universe would be chaotic. But these laws do operate in the same manner, day in and day out.

God has also instituted certain unbreakable laws of right, or correct, thinking, which we call the laws of logic. One is known as the law of noncontradiction. First we'll look at what it says, and then we'll see what it means.

It says, "Two contradictory, or opposite, truth claims cannot both be true at the same time and in the same sense." Here's an example of how it works: The contradiction to "God exists" is "God does not exist," and the law of noncontradiction says these two truth claims can't both be true—God can't both exist and not exist. If you're reading this book right now, you can't *not* be reading this book right now. If your birthday is January 1, 1994, it can't also be true that your birthday is not January 1, 1994. When you really think about this, it just makes sense.

Why is this so important, and why should you spend your time on it? Because while it's common today to maintain that all belief systems are equally true, or that no belief system has any "truth advantage" over any other, the fact is that religions *contradict* each other at many major points.

For example, let's look at just three key Christian beliefs about Jesus: (1) Jesus is God; (2) Jesus has always been God; he did not at some point in time become God; (3) only Jesus is God; people are not God.

Here's the issue: Every other system of belief contradicts these claims. Hindus say Jesus is one of many men who've become God. Mormons believe that Jesus was a man before he became God, and that worthy Mormons can become gods one day also. Muslims esteem Jesus as one of Allah's great prophets, but they do not believe he is God. Buddhists hold Jesus to be one of many remarkable teachers. Judaism does not believe Jesus is God. Each religion believes something contradictory about who Jesus is or who he claimed to be.

This is where the law of noncontradiction becomes crucial. It tells us that someone is right and someone is wrong about Jesus. All these ideas about him cannot be right, because they are contradictory. If Christianity is true—if what it says about Jesus is true—then all these other belief systems are wrong.

To find out which truth claim matches reality, we must examine the facts, the data—the evidence. While we won't always come to the same conclusion, we cannot pretend all the choices are correct. They can't be, when they're contradictory. So we will find that we are compelled to make a choice. Either God exists or he doesn't. Either Jesus is eternally and uniquely God or he is not.

We'll refer to the law of noncontradiction several times in this book. You might want to mark this page in case you want to come back to it at some point. Pretending that contradictory truth claims can be true in the same way at the same time is not only sloppy thinking, it's also wrong thinking.

Three Reasons Why We Need to Have the Right View of Truth

Truth Affects Our Daily Life

If truth were merely what is true for you, then all of life would be chaotic bedlam. How could anyone say *anything* and expect you to take them seriously? Why should anyone teach—why should anyone ever take a test, if no answer key exists? It's naïve and unrealistic to believe that anything and everything is true. If that were the case, then *nothing* would be true.

Truth Affects Our Eternal Life

If truth is only my set of opinions, then there is no objective reality. If that were the case, we would have no basis for believing we can know anything true about God, about life, or about what happens after we die. It's not just the here and now that's at stake. Eternity itself hangs in the balance.

The Bible Makes Truth Claims

The Bible has much to say about truth. It claims that the God of the Bible is the one true God, the God of truth. It claims that his way and his Word are true (e.g., see Psalm 31:5; 119:30, 43).

Jesus claimed he is the truth: "I am the way and the truth and the life. No one comes to the Father except through me" (John 14:6). Seventy-eight times in the New Testament Jesus explicitly claimed to be speaking the truth. And God's Holy

21

Spirit is called "the Spirit of truth," who reveals the truth to people (John 15:26; see also John 19:35; Acts 28:25).

The Bible says the good news about Jesus Christ is true (Galatians 2:14) and that we can learn and know the truth (see Acts 24:8; 2 Corinthians 4:2). It claims to offer the answers to our most significant questions, the solutions to our most crucial problems, the fixes for all our failures, and the provisions for our every true need.

The Bible, then, does not leave itself open to being placed in the category of "books that contain intriguing ethics" or "sources of some decent ideas about how to construct our own reality." It doesn't say it may have some value for someone, depending on their circumstances and individual perspectives. It says it is God's Word; it says it is the truth. So either it is the truth or it is not.

A Frequent Perception, or Accusation

Many people think Christians are closed-minded. When they hear believers say, for instance, "Jesus is the only way to God," they come to the conclusion that Christians aren't open to truth, or are against learning.

But think about this. An atheist's claim that there's no God is just as closed-minded. And the claim that there are many ways to God has the same degree of closed-mindedness. Each is a declaration that something is true and that, by definition, what contradicts or opposes it is false.

Every truth claim is narrow. Why? Because truth itself is narrow. If you jump off a tall building with no ability to remain aloft, you will fall to the ground, yet no one would say belief in the law of gravity is being narrow-minded.

All religious truth claims are equally narrow as well, for all such claims maintain that they are true and that opposing claims are false. A person is no more closed-minded for saying God exists than for saying he does not exist. The fact is that one of the statements is true; therefore, the opposing view is false. Believing either one automatically excludes believing the other.

Christians should be open to all truth, since all truth is God's—all truth flows from his nature. Not one single aspect of truth pops up and surprises God, for he is the source of all truth. Believers need not fear that somehow a new truth will come along and undermine the God of truth.

Christians ought to be willing to look at all the facts, all the evidence. We're to be closed-minded only when it comes to accepting something that is untrue, does not match reality, or does not tell it like it is. Let's say: *Bring on the truth!*

What We've Learned

1. Truth is what matches the facts, what corresponds to reality.
2. Contradictions (or opposites) cannot both be true at the same time and in the same sense. If a statement is true, its contradiction is false.

These two statements lay the foundation for our next challenge regarding the existence of God.

3

God (Part I)

Challenge #2: "God Does Not Exist"

Potential problem: Christianity rests upon God's existence. If God does not exist, Christianity is false.

If you were to take a poll today and ask a random group of people if they believe there's a God, aside from those who say they don't know, naturally you'd get two opposing answers. Some would answer yes, others no.

Many today openly and strongly deny that God exists. They do this for many reasons, one of which is that they don't think there's any evidence for his existence. Lacking that, they conclude they would be foolish to believe a God is out there somewhere.

If you asked those who affirmed God's existence to explain what *kind* of God exists, you'd discover that not everyone who believes in God agrees on what he's like (his nature). The poll's end product would show how much disparity there is about the existence and nature of God.

Our task in the coming chapters will be to answer two main questions:

1. What is the evidence that God exists?
2. Which god does the evidence point to? Is it a match for the God of the Bible or for a different god?

The answers to these two questions are foundational, because if there is no God, then there is no Word of God, Jesus is not the Son of God, Jesus did not die for our sins or rise from the dead; all the tenets of the Christian faith would collapse. The same is true as to God's nature. If the evidence supports a god other than the God of the Bible, then believers have misplaced their trust.

We will approach the question of God's existence as a sleuth would seek to solve a mystery. When a detective needs to determine whether someone was in a certain location, he looks for clues—such as fingerprints.

Think about the trail of evidence your fingerprints leave behind. They mark everything you touch from the time you rise in the morning until you're back in bed at night. From every dish, light switch, door handle, or book, to your keyboard, steering wheel, cell phone, and toothbrush, your prints provide evidence of where you've been throughout the day. Seeking an answer to the question "Does God exist?" we can look for whether God has left his prints on the universe to show us he is there. In this chapter and the next, we'll examine the evidence that demonstrates that God does exist, and he has left behind his fingerprints as proof.

Some Christians don't think it's important to consider the evidence for God's existence. They say it's enough just to have faith that he's there. But many nonbelievers are not persuaded or swayed by a faith-alone argument for God, since they believe they have evidence for God's *non*existence. The question is, which position does the evidence support? Do the facts support a belief in God? Can we demonstrate convincingly that the God of the Bible is there?

Your Worldview Will Determine What You Believe About God

Every person has something called a *worldview*, which is simply the way one views and understands life. It's how we answer the big questions, such as:

- Where did we come from? Are we a byproduct of evolutionary processes, or were we created by God?

- Why are we here? Does life have any meaning or purpose, or are we born only to die?

- What happens to us after we die? Is heaven real? Is hell real? Or do we simply cease to exist? Is reincarnation a possibility? Do we get a second, third, or fourth chance after we die?

Sooner or later everyone forms an answer to these questions. Even little children by the time they start school have begun to develop their own responses. Your answers on matters like these will determine your worldview, and how you think about God, about his nature, and about life in general.

There are a number of contradictory worldviews. We'll examine four of the most common: atheism, deism, pantheism, and theism. Our goal is to ascertain which view of God makes the most sense and has the most supportive evidence.

Atheism

Atheism is the worldview that claims there is no God, no matter how you think of him or what you choose to call him. There's no higher power, no Absolute Being, no universal Life Force, no World Spirit that originated the universe. Atheists believe the universe is eternal; it did not have a beginning and won't have an end. They say everything we observe (stars, space, planets [including earth]) has always existed—nothing was created. Thus humanity is the result of the blind natural forces that by chance combined in such a way as to form life on earth. Consequently, there's no particular purpose or reason for our existence. We're born, we live for a time, then we die, and life is over—there's no afterlife at all.

Deism

Deism is a word we don't hear much anymore. But many people today have chosen it as their worldview, whether or not they call it by that name. Deists believe there is a God who created the universe, so unlike atheists, they believe the universe is not eternal; it had a beginning. Deists also believe God created people; we're not the result of blind evolutionary forces. However, deists maintain that after creating, God simply withdrew and left us here on our own; he's no longer directly involved in his creation.

Deists, then, don't believe in miracles. The deistic God is inaccessible, remote, and not directly involved. He does not, and will not, intervene in our lives.

Thomas Jefferson believed there is a God but did not believe in miracles. To make Scripture match reality as he perceived it, Jefferson got out his Bible, took a pair of scissors, and cut out every reference to the supernatural in the four Gospels. Then he published his own version of them, which is still in print today, known as *The Jefferson Bible* (or *The Life and Morals of Jesus of Nazareth*). Because he removed every miracle account, his book ends with these words: "There laid they Jesus, and rolled a great stone to the door of the sepulcher, and departed"[1] (no mention is made of the resurrection).

Pantheism

The pantheistic view of life is popular today, though (like deism) the term *pantheism* is not often used in conversation. It comes from a combination of two other words: *pan*, which means "all," and *theos*, which means "God." Together they describe a worldview maintaining that everything we see— every animal, insect, tree, stream, person—is imbued with a divine god-force. So nature itself and every living creature is, in essence, part of God. One expression that illustrates pantheism is this: "There is a god, and you are him."

However, the god of pantheism is not a god to whom you pray or with whom you have a relationship. *You* are god. We *all* are.

Many saw the movie *Avatar*—a box-office smash from its time of release—primarily because of the new (at the time) 3-D technology. Relatively few seemed to recognize, though, that the film's basic worldview is pantheism.

The movie is about the Na'vi, a tall, blue-skinned tribe who live in very large trees and worship a nature goddess they call Eywa. Eywa inhabits the trees, the streams, and all of the forest. Na'vi goddess-worship actually is the worship of nature; Eywa's force flows through every aspect of creation. From the pantheistic perspective, all of nature is part of "God."

Many Americans have adhered to some form of pantheism, especially since the 1960s, when what became known as the New Age Movement became popular. Among the convictions of New Agers is that they, like the rest of nature, are part of God and that a time is coming when humankind will take its final evolutionary step (or leap). This will not be a biological transformation but a spiritual one; it will be achieved when we all recognize that we are god. Many who claim to have this godlike force within are waiting for the rest of us to come to the same conclusion and at last usher in an age of universal love, harmony, and peace.

Theism

Theism, the final worldview we'll examine,[2] contends that there is one and only one eternal God who created the entire universe—everything that exists. The universe is not eternal; it has not always been here. Rather, it came into being "in the beginning," when God spoke it into existence.

It's clear from the start that theism contradicts the three previously defined views. Theism contradicts atheism in denying that the universe is eternal and in rejecting the idea that life, including humankind, evolved from primordial soup by chance via the blind laws of nature. Theists assert that we are a unique act of a Creator God who *began* the universe.

Theism contradicts deism in affirming that God has remained actively involved in human matters; he did not create the universe and then walk away. We can pray to him for help and guidance. He can choose to answer prayers by natural or by supernatural (miraculous) means.

Theism stands in contradiction to pantheism in that the theistic God is not man, and man does not share in God's nature. God created man, but he did not create man out of himself. In contrast to pantheism, "There is a God, and we are *not* him." He is outside of us. We are not God and, theists believe, will never become God.

A Summary of Four Key Worldviews

1. *Atheism:* The universe is eternal. There is no God and no miracles.
2. *Deism:* The God who created the universe is absent and inactive. There are no miracles.
3. *Pantheism:* God made the universe out of himself. There are no miracles, since God is in all; all is part of God.
4. *Theism:* God created everything that is by speaking it into existence; he is an active God who has done, can do, and will do miracles.

We begin to see substantial contradictions between these worldviews. Does God exist or not? If he does exist, does he miraculously intervene in human affairs? Did he create us out of himself or out of nothing? Are we part of God, or are we a separate creative act that does not share in God's nature?

For each contradiction, someone is right and someone is wrong, for reality's unbreakable law of noncontradiction says that contradictory truth claims cannot both be true at the same time and in the same sense.

Nothing is as important as what you think or believe about God, for this will determine what you believe about truth, about where we came from, about why we're here, and about what happens to us after we die.

So we'll be comparing these worldviews and asking, "Which best explains the real world?" Which best matches the evidence we'll examine in the chapters ahead?

God Isn't Santa Claus

There is one more popular view of God that should be mentioned. Some people think of God somewhat like Santa: You climb onto his lap, tell him you've been good, and then say what you want him to do for you.

If you're a "good" person, Santa (God) will give you what you want. If you are not so good, he'll tell you to try harder and come back next year.

Many people think if they're "good," God will give them what they request, treat them well, and eventually bring them to heaven (that's where "good" people go).

The problem is, this does not match the biblical God—a holy God whose standard we cannot meet on our own. God *doesn't* give us what we deserve, and for that we can be eternally thankful. We pray to him (and love him and serve him) because *he* is good, not because we are.

Three Basic Arguments for God's Existence

We will consider three primary lines of evidence, each of which provides support for the existence of a theistic God.

1. Science provides us with evidence that the universe had a beginning. Therefore, Someone, or Something, must have brought it into existence; that is, *began* it. The key question is: "Who or what brought the universe into existence?" (Someone/Something, Who/What are capped when indicating or referring to an ultimate being, i.e., God.)

2. Science also provides ample evidence that the universe was designed. Only a personal being, or a designer, can design something. Thus, if Someone or Something designed the universe, Who or What designed it?

3. There's evidence too for the existence of a universal moral law. As all laws must be made or passed by a lawmaker, we must ask: Who is the lawmaker that made or passed the universal moral law?

We'll consider the first argument now and the other two in chapter 4.

A Beginning: First Argument for God's Existence

The first argument for the existence of God can be stated like this:

1. Everything that had a beginning, had a Beginner (or Causer).

2. The universe had a beginning (it's not eternal).

3. Therefore, the universe had a Beginner (or Causer).

If the first two points are true, the third point is automatically true.

First Point: Everything That Had a Beginning Had a Beginner

One of the most basic laws of science is known as the law of causality. This law says, essentially, "Anything that had a *beginning* was caused by something outside of itself." Another way to say this is that if something had a beginning, then Someone/Something had to bring it into existence. If we can show that the universe had a beginning, then the law of causality will demand that a Beginner of some kind created or caused it. This principle is so foundational that one of history's most famous skeptics, David Hume, said, "I never asserted so absurd a proposition as that anything might arise without a cause."[3]

The following all demonstrate how this law operates: animals, insects, trees, plants, chairs, books, ships, and jet airplanes all had a beginning; they all have a cause. Vehicles are caused by a variety of people who plan, design, produce, and assemble them. Computers are caused by people who design hardware and write software. Buildings are caused by architects, contractors, carpenters, and many others. It's not difficult to come up with a very long list of things that had a beginning and are therefore subject to the law of causality that requires a beginner/causer for each.

Think about the song from *The Sound of Music* that tells us nothing can come from nothing. *Why* can't something come from nothing? Because *nothing* is just that—it's nothing! Something, or Someone, must begin or cause everything that comes into being.

The law of causality proves our first point: Everything that had a beginning had a Beginner (or Causer).

Second Point: The Universe Had a Beginning
(It Is Not Eternal)

Next, we must ask ourselves if the universe had a beginning. Was there a beginning to stars, planets, galaxies, time, space, matter, energy, and life itself? Or does atheism correctly maintain that the universe is eternal? If the latter is true, then no Beginner is required and our argument fails to provide evidence for God's existence.

Two pieces of evidence help to show that the universe had a beginning and therefore is not eternal—Someone or Something had to cause or "begin" it.

THE SECOND LAW

The second law of thermodynamics says that the universe is running out of usable energy. This principle is relatively simple to understand.

Think of iPods, which are made (or begun, or created) by designers and assemblers. If you buy a new one, naturally you'll want to use it right away. But an iPod won't operate without a charged battery, so you must plug it in for a few hours first. Then you can turn it on, and presto! It works.

As you listen to music (or view movies or photos), the iPod's battery gradually loses its charge and increasingly runs down. At some point, without a recharge, it will stop working, having "run out of usable energy."

Here's the point: The iPod, its battery and energy, had a beginning. And from the time you first use it, the energy stored in it starts to deplete. Its available energy will eventually run out. This means there was a limited amount of energy in your iPod battery from the beginning.

The universe in which we live is very similar (though it has no docking station or USB connector). That its usable energy is running down means it had a beginning. It's *not* eternal—if it were, then it would have unlimited, inexhaustible energy that would never run out or end, because eternity never runs out or ends. Like an iPod, the universe had to have a beginning.

"THE BIG BANG"

Second, the universe is expanding as it would if it were the result of a gigantic explosion that happened at the *beginning* of the universe. That is, the universe is expanding from a point of beginning.

Early in the twentieth century, Albert Einstein developed a theory that said the universe—time, space, matter, and energy—all had a beginning. At that time, science lacked sufficient hard evidence to demonstrate that he was correct—and, in fact, Einstein wasn't even convinced his theory was accurate. But subsequent years brought the discovery of much supporting data.

The trail of evidence showing a beginning to our universe started to accumulate in the 1920s with the astronomer Edwin Hubble. Using one of that era's largest telescopes, Dr. Hubble (for whom the Hubble Space Telescope is named) took a series of photos of nearby galaxies over a period of time. Under careful examination, his pictures showed something unexpected: The galaxies were moving away from earth at a very high speed.

These images provided the first hard scientific evidence that the universe was expanding. Stranger still, they seemed to indicate that these galaxies were expanding from a single point of *beginning* somewhere in the distant past. Scientists who grasped the implications of Hubble's discovery understood it as evidence that the universe is not eternal; these images also indicated that the universe *came into being* by means of an event resembling a massive explosion. Once there was nothing, and then *BANG!* The universe exploded into reality at a single point, a point from which the galaxies appeared to be still expanding.

If this were true, the "explosion," which came to be known as *The Big Bang*, would have been extremely hot. All explosions give off some amount of heat, whether they result from a firecracker or an atomic bomb. Imagine the heat produced in an explosion so massive as to have begun the universe.

If the universe did result from an explosion, there should be some detectable heat left over. A blast of such magnitude would have been fantastically hot, and heat leaves a "signature." If you've seen heat waves rising from asphalt on a sunny day, you've seen evidence that the roadway has heated. Those waves will continue to radiate for a time even after the sun goes down while the pavement cools.

Scientists knew that evidence of the original explosion in the form of heat (or radiation) should still exist. And they found it in 1965.

While trying to fine-tune a sensitive radio-receiving device, Dr. Arno Penzias and Dr. Robert Wilson inadvertently discovered an unusual kind of heat signature in the form of radiation. Puzzled, they began to study it and came to realize that the radiation they'd uncovered was being picked up from every direction in the universe. No matter where they pointed their receiver, the signature showed up, and it was constant—it was the same day and night all throughout the year.

At first they didn't know exactly how to explain what they'd found. But over time scientists began to see that this signature matched the radiation from a colossal blast. It was, in fact, evidence of the explosion that marked the *origin* of the universe. In 1978, Penzias and Wilson received the Nobel Prize in Physics for their discovery.

Neither of these men was a believer, yet Penzias said the easiest way to explain their finds was to say "the universe was created *out of nothing*, in an instant, and continues to expand. . . . [What we found] is a creation *out of nothing*, the appearance *out of nothing* of a universe"[4] (emphasis added).

That statement, comparable to the biblical creation narrative, is a remarkable declaration from someone who did not believe the account as recorded in Genesis. Carefully read the verses below to see how much these discoveries concur with Scripture.

- Einstein's theory, which came to be accepted, says that there was a beginning to time, space, matter, and energy. The Bible says: "In the *beginning* [time] God created the *heavens* [space] and the *earth* [matter]" (Genesis 1:1); "In the *beginning* [time], Lord, you laid the foundations of the *earth* [matter], and the *heavens* [space] are the work of your hands" (Hebrews 1:10).

- Hubble showed that the universe is expanding. The Bible says: "He [God] alone *stretches out the heavens* and treads on the waves of the sea" (Job 9:8); "He *stretches out the heavens* like a canopy, and spreads them out like a tent to live in" (Isaiah 40:22).

As more and more evidence was found, scientists became increasingly convinced that the universe had a beginning—it hasn't always been there; it isn't eternal. The agnostic Robert Jastrow, NASA's first chairman of lunar exploration, the founding director of its Goddard Institute for Space Studies, and Dartmouth professor of earth sciences, said in *God and the Astronomers*:

> Now we see how the astronomical evidence leads to a biblical view of the origin of the world. . . . The chain of events leading to man commenced suddenly and sharply at a definite moment in time, in a flash of light and energy.[5]

Further, the accumulated data showed the universe to have exploded into being *out of nothing*. But how could this be? How could everything we see come from nothing? It couldn't; again, nothing cannot cause something. Someone or Something *caused* ("began") the universe. Wilson said:

> Certainly there was something that set it all off. . . . If you are religious, I can't think of a better theory of the origin of the universe to match with than Genesis.[6]

The fact that the universe had a beginning isn't new information. The Bible said long ago that the Beginner was God himself.

> In the *beginning* you laid the foundations of the earth, and the heavens are the work of your hands. (Psalm 102:25)

> You are worthy, our Lord and God, to receive glory and honor and power, for you created all things, and by your will they were created and have their being. (Revelation 4:11)

What We've Learned

The Logical Conclusion

We have given evidence that proves our first two statements.

1. Everything that had a beginning has a Beginner (or Causer)—the law of causality demands it. Nothing causes (or pops into being by) itself.
2. The second law of thermodynamics, Hubble's law, and the cumulative evidence for The Big Bang, demonstrate that the universe had a beginning.

The truth of the first two statements establishes the truth of the third, which is their necessary conclusion:

3. The universe had a Beginner.

The scientific discoveries of the past hundred years have uncovered some of the Beginner's "fingerprints," and the Bible identifies him as God.

As to his existence, in the next chapter we'll look at two more proofs:

1. God's fingerprints can be found in the design of the universe.
2. God's fingerprints can be found in the moral law that exists in human hearts and minds.

Why Such a Focus on Science?

In this chapter we've relied on what science says about the universe's beginning and on the laws surrounding that occurrence. Yet some Christians, skeptical of science, shy away from scientific evidence. Some even worry that a scientific discovery may come along that will seem to contradict the Bible.

However, the God of the Bible is the God of truth; *all* truth comes from him. This means no matter where truth is found, it is from God, from out of his very nature. It is his fingerprint, left behind to point us to him.

In 1948, the astronomer Peter Stoner wrote about the scientific evidence for Christianity:

Thirty-five years ago [looking back to 1913] astronomy and the account of creation as recorded in the first chapter of Genesis differed in many points. . . . But year after year advances were made in science, which resulted in an improved agreement between Genesis and astronomy. Within the past generation, *not a single instance* is known where astronomy has agreed with Genesis and later changed its mind[7] (emphasis added).

Dr. Stoner wrote these words long before the discovery of the bulk of contemporary evidence supporting belief in

---

"The Big Bang"

The belief that the universe exploded into existence at a single point in time became known as "The Big Bang." This should not be confused with how the term is used in macro-evolutionary theory—here it refers to an initial explosion by which time, space, matter, and energy, in an ordered manner, were brought into existence out of nothing. Many scientists, teachers, pastors, and philosophers use this expression to describe how God created everything (compare to Genesis 1:1).

Genesis 1 and The Big Bang. There have been many new discoveries since his time, and what he wrote in 1948 is still true: "Within the past generation, *not a single instance* is known where astronomy has agreed with Genesis and later changed its mind."

God (Part II)

Challenge #2: "God Does Not Exist"

Potential problem: Christianity rests on God's existence. If God does not exist, Christianity is false.

We've just seen some of the evidence for the existence of God. In this chapter we will look at two other areas: design in the universe, and the universal moral law found in the heart and minds of all people.

Design: A Second Argument for God's Existence

Here's how we'll present our argument:

1. Every complex design has a designer.
2. Everywhere we look in the universe we find evidence of complex design.
3. Therefore, the universe had a Designer.

Again, if the first two statements are true, then so is the third. Before going further, let's specify what we mean by *complex design*. Here are three tests we'll use to determine whether or not something is truly designed as opposed to being the result of natural forces.

1. Is it simple or complex?
2. Is it just orderly or does it also convey some kind of information?
3. Does it seem to have a purpose?

Three Tests for Design

Test #1: Whether It's Simple or Complex

Let's look at an example of what we mean by *simple* and *complex*. A mountain, even if picturesque and beautiful, has a *simple* form that's explained by the forces of nature—wind, rain, ice, and snow, for instance, have shaped its outline. By contrast, specifically, picture Mount Rushmore, which famously and intricately displays the faces of four American presidents. These very complex features cannot be the result of natural causes—even if we didn't know who caused the design, obviously someone planned and designed the faces we see.

Test #2: Is It Just Orderly or Does It Also Convey Information?

Here's an example of *order*:

DXDXDXDXDXDXDXDXDX

In this illustration, everything is organized into an orderly pattern. But there's no information—it makes no sense and conveys no message.

Now look at the two images below. The first is the result of wind and water (both natural causes). The other has a *message*; it conveys *information*.

Information is a mark of design, and design is a mark of an intelligent being. In the case of the universe, we'll call the intelligent being the Designer.

For one more example, first picture a canyon that over time has been eroded into certain patterns. Then picture a rock wall with hieroglyphics that depict birds and people and homes. The features of the canyon are the result of time, wind, water, and erosion. The hieroglyphics were made by design. They were designed by a designer, and convey information (even if we don't understand it).

TEST #3: WHETHER IT HAS A PURPOSE

Sometimes we can't be, or aren't, sure about a design's intended purpose. For example, people have not always understood the meaning or purpose of hieroglyphics. But they did know it served a purpose: it was conveying some kind of information. Once the code was broken, we could understand the meaning and therefore the purpose. In the case above of the message in the sand, the purpose is pretty clear. Someone wants someone else to know that they love them.

With this understanding of design, we can begin to establish our first point.

First Point: Every Complex Design Has a Designer

We don't need to search long or hard for examples of design. Among the nearly countless things people design are homes, buildings, bridges, factories, cars, engines, planes, watches, computers, cameras, paintings, sculptures, and clothes. All of these need someone who plans them out, whether an architect, a painter, an engineer, or other. In fact, though certainly some designs work better than others, everything people make is designed.

This point is easy to prove. Everything that's complex, conveys information, and has a purpose is designed. And where we find design, we'll always find a designer.

Second Point: The Universe Is Filled With Evidence of Complex Design

Just like in our everyday world, in the universe we find design virtually everywhere we look. To determine whether it was designed, and thus whether there's a Designer, we'll apply our three tests to it.

Remember, we are looking for evidence of God's existence. Did he leave his fingerprints in the design of the universe?

APPLYING TEST #1 FOR DESIGN: SIMPLE OR COMPLEX?

Consider the cell. Every life form, including plants and animals, is made up of cells. The human body is composed of many different types, such as blood cells, nerve cells, muscle cells, and bone cells.

Until recently these cells were essentially a mystery to scientists. Because the early microscopes weren't powerful enough to see inner cellular details, cells appeared to be very simple. But modern technology has shown scientists the details inside a given cell, and initially they were stunned to see how complex even the simplest cell is. We know today that a single cell is made up of multiple complex parts.

Consider your own body, which has various internal parts—such as the stomach, heart, brain, liver, kidneys—we call *organs*. Each has a unique duty to perform. While our organs interact with one another, they each perform their own function as well.

Cells also have parts known as *organelles*, or "little organs." These also interact, and each has a job. For instance, some organelles clean up the cell, others help make proteins, and others help the cell divide.

The cell is the simplest of life forms, yet the more scientists learn about it the more they see its complexity. Each and every cell provides us with evidence of complex design.

APPLYING TEST #2 FOR DESIGN: ORDER ONLY, OR INFORMATION?

In 1953, James Watson and Francis Crick discovered DNA. Those letters stand for deoxyribonucleic acid, which is found inside each individual cell of every plant, animal, and human being. Visually, DNA can be pictured like two sides of a twisting ladder, steps (rungs) and all.

DNA is to the cell what our brain is to our body. It's where the cell stores all the information necessary for it (the cell) to function.

The more we study DNA, the more we realize how much info is stored there. Like a highly detailed manual, DNA tells each cell what to make and how to make it. Hair, muscle, nerves, blood, bone cells—DNA runs them all.

DNA also contains instructions that tell each cell how to replicate itself and when to divide. For life to continue, DNA must reproduce itself daily inside special cells in a person's body, since cells do not always have a very long life; that is, some cells exist for a short time and then die.[1] If cells didn't know how to divide, they'd eventually die out, and ultimately so would we. Without DNA and all the information it contains, life would not be possible.

DNA works like extremely complex software. It cannot be seen by the human eye, yet it stores more data in a smaller space than our most advanced supercomputers. The DNA in the human brain contains more information than hundreds of encyclopedia volumes.

DNA certainly meets our first two tests: It's highly complex and contains detailed information. But this raises some questions. What's the source of the information and instructions stored in DNA? What determines how its messages are sent? How does the cell's machinery know to build proteins? Who or what tells its machinery how to divide?

There aren't many choices as to the answers. We know that information comes only from a mind; all information is the result of someone's mind, somewhere. Look at any email, article, book, or code—someone had to plan and write it. There is an intelligent mind behind each one.

But DNA is far more than an email or a book. It's a phenomenal amount of organized data. All these marks of design mean somewhere a Designer is behind it.

Stephen C. Meyer, a founder of the Center for Science and Culture (part of the Discovery Institute), said there is a mind behind the information found in DNA "that's far greater than our own—a conscious, purposeful, rational, intelligent designer, who's amazingly creative. There's no getting around it."[2]

Bill Gates said, "DNA is like a software program, only much more complex than anything we've ever devised."[3]

APPLYING TEST #3 FOR DESIGN: DOES IT HAVE
A PURPOSE?

Our final test will show the degree to which the universe has been designed for a purpose: that of sustaining human life. We've noted that if something is designed, it is normally designed for a purpose, even if just for fun.

Consider cars. They're all designed, and their primary purpose is getting people from one place to another. Even so, today's cars are designed to do more. They're also designed to get us from one place to another safely, and in comfort, and with options and amenities. Car designers leave us with a lot of evidence that they want us to arrive securely while having enjoyed the trip.

Just think of all the things designed into today's cars. Seats for our comfort. Air bags for our safety. GPS for keeping us on track. Multimedia centers (with premium sound and even HD) for our enjoyment. Data panels for accurate and precise information. Wheels and a finely tuned engine to ensure we finish our journey in good shape. Great care is being taken to design cars for easier, safer, and more enjoyable road travel.

The Universe Appears to Be Designed for Life

The universe also seems to have been planned and designed with a particular purpose in mind: to sustain life on earth. In fact, it has been designed and prepared as though we were expected to show up. Let's look at eight supporting facts.

1. THE BEGINNING OF THE UNIVERSE WAS DESIGNED
   FOR LIFE

That from the very beginning the universe was suited to allow for life can be seen in the fact that its original expansion rate was perfectly balanced. If the universe had expanded faster than it did, no planets could have formed. If no planets could form, there would be no earth. No earth? No life on earth. If the universe had expanded more slowly, it would have eventually collapsed back on itself. Again, no earth. No earth? No life on earth. The rate of expansion was perfectly designed to ensure life's survival. Who planned and controlled this perfectly designed expansion rate? A Designer did.

2. THE LAWS OF THE UNIVERSE ARE SUITED FOR LIFE

The universe operates according to a set of laws—such as the law of gravity and the speed of light. These laws were finely tuned right from the start to allow for life. If you were to change any of them, life as we know it could not exist on earth. Steven Hawking, one of our time's most brilliant scientists, said, "The remarkable fact is that . . . [these laws] seem to have been very finely adjusted to make possible the development of life."[4] Anthony Flew, perhaps the most famous atheist of the twentieth century, said that for life to arise at all, the universe had to be "'adjusted' in a particular way."[5] If there'd been no fine-tuning of these laws, there'd be no life. Who fine-tuned them? Only a Designer could have.

3. OUR GALAXY IS SUITED FOR LIFE

There are billions of galaxies in the universe. Also, there are different kinds of galaxies. We live in a spiral galaxy, the kind most suited for life. Other kinds, like elliptical or irregular galaxies, cannot support life. Some are too close to each other. Others are too hot or too unstable. Only our kind of galaxy provides life with the best chance of survival.[6]

4. OUR LOCATION IN OUR GALAXY IS POSITIONED FOR LIFE

Our planet is located in a spiral galaxy known as the Milky Way. Spiral galaxies look like they have "arms," and we are located in a perfect spot between two spiral "arms." If we were closer to our galaxy's "arms," the earth could not have formed. If we were too close to the galaxy's nucleus, life could not survive the deadly radiation bursts and gamma rays found there.

Furthermore, earth is located in what's known as a "safe zone," a narrow area outside of which life cannot exist. For example, if we were any closer to our sun, we'd burn up. If we were any farther from it, even by as little as 2 to 5 percent, we'd freeze to death.

Is this the result of chance, of luck? Or did a Master Designer plan this because he had a deliberate purpose: to create a place for life to survive and flourish?

5. OUR SUN IS PERFECTLY POSITIONED FOR LIFE ON EARTH[7]

Scientists used to think our sun was pretty ordinary. But today we know it's actually unique. For life to survive on a planet like earth, its sun must be a certain size (not too big or too small). And it must have a very precise temperature (not too hot or too cold). Any temperature extreme and life would burn up or freeze. Our sun is exactly the right size and the right temperature for life on earth to survive. Our sun is designed for human life.

6. NEARBY PLANETS (LIKE JUPITER) HELP LIFE ON EARTH TO SURVIVE[8]

Jupiter is a huge planet. Because of its size, it draws asteroids and comets away from us. If Jupiter were any smaller or any farther away, comets would come into the inner solar system and eventually collide with earth, destroying large sections of our planet and eventually all life on earth. Without a planet like Jupiter, life on earth could not survive.

7. Our moon is perfectly situated for life on earth[9]

We also have the perfect moon—it's the right size and distance from earth to keep our orbit stable. Without this particular moon, our orbit would be unstable, making life here impossible.

It also regulates our tides. If the moon were larger, tides would swamp much of the land. Our moon is designed to allow for human life to survive.

8. Our planet is perfectly suitable for human life[10]

Earth itself has an ideal balance of water and land. It has enough plant life to provide us with food. It has enough fresh water to sustain life. Its atmosphere is perfectly balanced to sustain human life. If our atmosphere were thicker, the sun's rays couldn't keep it warm enough. Earth would be too cold; we couldn't grow food. If our atmosphere were thinner, we'd be bombarded by harmful rays from the sun. The earth would turn into a desert. We wouldn't be able to grow the food necessary for survival. Even our atmosphere appears to be designed for life on earth.

Scientist and mathematician Freeman Dyson said, "The more I examine the universe, and the details of its architecture, the more evidence I find that the universe in some sense must have known we were coming."[11] The Designer not only knew we were coming, he prepared the earth for us, and we can see some of the fingerprints that prove it.

More than thirty separate features had to be perfectly balanced in order for there to be life on earth. This means Someone had to plan and design all this. And as we've already seen, where we find design we'll always find a Designer.

Astronomer Robert Jastrow reached the following conclusion: "This universe was made, [it] was designed, for man to live in."[12]

The Necessary Conclusion

We have shown that the first two points are true:

1. Every complex design has a designer.
2. Everywhere we look in the universe, we find evidence of complex design.

We've found God's fingerprints in the design of the universe. From the single cell, to DNA, to the planning for human life, we see design everywhere. The entire universe was designed by a Designer, an intelligent being of great power who designed it with human life—with us—in mind.

Because the first two points are true, this is the necessary conclusion:

3. Therefore, the universe had a Designer.

The final piece of evidence we'll examine is the universal moral law.

Universal Moral Law: A Third Argument for God's Existence

No matter where we live there are laws. Every city, county, state, and nation has laws. We find laws at home, at school, at work. Parents "lay down the law." A host of laws impact what we can and can't do in many aspects of daily life. And some group (a council, a board of supervisors, a committee, or a congress) passes each law.

Our question for this section, however, doesn't have to do with man-made laws. We're asking whether there's evidence of a universal *moral* law. To answer, let's define our terms.

Law refers to certain requirements that must be followed. If we don't follow them, we face consequences. Not all man-made laws are passed on the basis of what's good or bad—sometimes they just dictate the decisions we make so as to not face a negative consequence. For example, on which side of the road should people drive? The answer depends on what country you're in. The choice wasn't made on the basis of which side is good or bad, but on the basis of *custom* and on what made sense to a particular group of people.

A moral law differs from a custom. Custom is the way people *do* behave. Morals refer to how they *ought* to behave. The question for this section is: "Are there any morals on which everyone agrees?" If so, where did they come from?

Here's how our argument will go:

1. Every moral law has a moral lawmaker.
2. There is a universal moral law.
3. Therefore, there must be a universal Moral Lawmaker.

If the first two points are true, then the third point is automatically true.

First Point: Every Law Has a Lawmaker

A few points will help to demonstrate this.

No Laws Happen on Their Own

No law pops into existence all by itself. Laws everywhere are made by someone. Someone passes every institutional, organizational, local, state, or national law. Laws are always passed by lawmakers.

Lawmakers Must Have the Authority to Pass Laws

You can't just decide on your own to pass a law and expect anyone to take it seriously. You also cannot enforce a penalty if someone breaks your own personal law. Unless you have some kind of authority or right to do so, no one has to obey your law.

The Authority for Every Law Must Come From Outside of You

Authority to pass a law must come from outside of you since, again, you have no right to pass a law on your own. Most lawmakers get their right to pass laws when they're elected or appointed to a certain position. The outside authority that gives someone the right to make laws is the body of people electing them or the person appointing them.

What about a dictator who seizes power and passes laws for a country? What's his "outside authority"? It can be an army, a police force, and/or a whole lot of threats, guns, and ammo. But no one has any authority to make and enforce laws without some kind of outside power or support.

Clearly, our first point is true: Every law has a lawmaker.

Second Point: There Is a Universal Moral Law

Some people say they don't believe there's a universal moral law. They don't think everyone agrees on certain rights and wrongs. A few points will show there are moral laws that, essentially, everyone agrees are right or wrong.

THE SAME BASIC MORAL CODE IS FOUND IN ALL CULTURES

First, the same basic moral code is found in all cultures. It's wrong to kill innocent people. It's wrong to steal something that belongs to someone else. It's wrong to lie. We should respect our parents. Rape, racism, and child pornography are wrong. There's basically universal agreement on these things.

When the U.S. captured Saddam Hussein and turned him over to the Iraqi government, his own people put him on trial. Virtually every nation found his actions to be morally wrong. There was no international outcry for him to be absolved. All peoples recognized his actions as criminal.

ALL PEOPLE BELIEVE CERTAIN RIGHTS SHOULD APPLY TO THEM

Second, all people believe they're entitled to certain rights. Now, looking at the list above, we can always come up with an exception. For example, what if I steal a loaf of bread to feed my starving family? What if I lie to save an innocent person? What if I don't respect my parents because they beat my younger siblings? And so on.

But think about this. There are certain things that virtually no one wants done to *them*. Don't injure or kill anyone I love. Don't lie to me. Don't lie about me. Don't take my stuff and call it yours. Don't treat me unfairly. Don't damage me. Don't abuse me or my family.

If anyone does these things to *us*, we get very upset. We don't say, "If it's okay with you, let's have this be the last time you set fire to my house" or "Is there any chance you'd mind not throwing grenades at my kids anymore?" We get angry! We get angry because someone has violated *our* moral code. While not everyone will agree that certain things are right or wrong for all people at all times in all places, the fact that some things are on virtually everyone's personal list of do's and don'ts is further evidence of a universal moral law.

ALL PEOPLE LIVE THEIR LIVES LIKE THERE IS A MORAL LAW

Third, all people live as though a moral law exists. Even those who deny its existence live as though it does. For instance, we've all apologized for things we've said or done that we knew instinctively weren't right.

ALL PEOPLE TALK LIKE THERE IS A MORAL LAW

Fourth, all people talk and act as though there is a moral law. We all tend to say that certain things are right and others are wrong. Anytime we do this, we're acknowledging a moral law. We say certain people are "better" than others. We affirm that it's right for people to be tried, convicted, and punished for committing certain crimes. Why would we say such things unless a moral law exists?

LIFE WOULD BE CHAOS WITHOUT A MORAL LAW

Fifth, life would be chaotic without a moral law. Think about what the world would be like if we did away with all moral laws. We'd be faced with the complete breakdown of law and order. If assault and murder, stealing, lying, and cheating were suddenly all fine, no one would be safe.

If there were no moral laws, there'd be no one to protect society, no one to detain and incarcerate criminals. If there were no one to hold terrorists, pirates, or even petty thieves accountable, society would collapse. Life as we know it would be impossible if there were no universal moral law.

MORAL LAWS ARE JUST PLAIN OBVIOUS

Finally, universal moral laws are plain-as-day obvious, because they are written on our conscience. Even if we damage our conscience by willfully and repeatedly overriding it, we all know when we've done something wrong. No matter when or where we live, we all know the difference between right and wrong. No nation in history has ever said unprovoked murder was fine or that acts of kindness called for punitive measures.

One of the twentieth century's most famous writers, C. S. Lewis, said of the universal moral law: "Human beings, all over the earth, have this curious idea that they ought to behave in a certain way, and cannot really get rid of it."[13] It's true. Deep down we all acknowledge the same moral law.

Moral law is just like truth. In chapter 2 we saw that we don't invent truth but rather discover it. The same is true of a universal moral law—we don't invent it, we just acknowledge it.

The existence of moral law doesn't mean everyone always agrees on every detail. Is it *ever* okay to murder? To lie? To steal? To take another's spouse? Different cultures make various exceptions at various times. All the same, all cultures generally believe murdering, lying, stealing, and committing adultery are wrong.

Neither do we always live by the moral law. Even so, it is the way we expect others to treat us. While we may choose to lie about or steal from others, we don't want them to lie about or steal from us.

The existence of a moral law means that there are basic principles of right and wrong and that we all know what they are—we cannot *not* know them. Around the world, people agree that certain basic moral laws exist.

The Logical Conclusion

We have shown that our first two points are true:

1. Every moral law has a moral lawmaker.
2. There is a universal moral law.

Because these two points are true:

3. Therefore, there must be a universal Moral Lawmaker.

Because there are universal morals that all people believe apply to others at all times and in all places, we must now ask: Who or what is their source?

We said at the start of this section that the authority to make laws must come from outside. So what or who is outside of all people, all cultures, at all times? This can only be God. Only an eternal being, such as God, can impose a moral law on all people, everywhere, and at all times. We cannot impose it on ourselves. We don't have the "outside" authority to do it. The Moral Lawmaker can only be God.

The fact of a universal moral law proves a universal Moral Lawmaker.

What We've Learned

We've examined two more facts providing evidence for the existence of God.

1. There is complex design virtually everywhere in the universe. Thus, there must be a Designer who planned and created it. Design doesn't just happen by itself—it doesn't result from time or chance. There's always a mind—an intelligence—a designer behind design.
2. There is a universal moral law. So there must be a Moral Lawmaker.

Next, we must ask ourselves: To which God does all this evidence point? Does it point to the God of the Bible, to the God of deism, or to the God of pantheism? That's the subject of our next chapter.

5

Which God?

Challenge #3: "If God Exists, He Isn't Necessarily the God of the Bible"

Potential Problem: The God of the Bible claims to be the only true God. *Does* the Beginner/Designer/Moral Lawmaker match the biblical God?

Now that we've looked at the evidence that God exists, we ask, "*Which* God does the evidence match?" In order to answer this, we must look at what God is like based on what we've learned:

• There is a Beginner.

• There is a Designer.

• There is a Moral Lawmaker.

We'll look at what the Bible says about the Beginner/Designer/Moral Lawmaker to see if our evidence agrees. We'll look at eight attributes, or characteristics, that the Beginner/Designer/Moral Lawmaker must possess.

What Kind of a Beginner?

Because the universe had a beginning, at least four things must be true of the Beginner.

Attribute #1: The Beginner Cannot Have a Cause

As we saw in chapter 3, everything that has a beginning must be caused by someone or something. But this can't be true of the Beginner. Why not?

If the Beginner needed a cause, we'd have to ask who or what caused (or created) him. Then we'd have to ask who or what caused whoever caused the beginner, and so on. Sooner or later there must be Someone or Something that did not have a cause. Otherwise we'd go back and back forever, trying to get to where it all got started. It has to start with Someone or Something that did not have a beginning, that did not have a cause.

This agrees with the Bible, which says that God is the Source (Cause) of *all* life. Therefore, he cannot have a cause. If something caused *God,* he would not be the source of all life; there would be another cause behind him.

> He is not served by human hands, as if he needed anything. Rather, he himself gives *everyone* life and breath and *everything* else. (Acts 17:25)

Question: "Who Made God?"

Answer: "Nobody made God." God does not need a cause, for he did not have a beginning. Not everything needs a cause—only what has a beginning does.

God is in a different *category* than we are. We're not eternal; God is, because the Beginner must be eternal.

God and humans have some points of similarity, but in many ways comparing God to a human is like comparing a spear of broccoli to a dog. They're both alive, but they're not the same—they're in different *categories*. One is a vegetable, the other is a mammal. Broccoli is not conscious; a dog is. A dog has feelings, can make sounds, and can relate to people; broccoli cannot. Broccoli can't learn; a dog can. They aren't in the same category. No one made God; he is uncreated.

From him and through him and for him are *all* things. (Romans 11:36)

In him *all* things were created: things in heaven and on earth, visible and invisible, whether thrones or powers or rulers or authorities; *all* things have been created through him and for him. (Colossians 1:16)

God is the source of all life, all space, all matter; he created everything. Accordingly, he must be uncaused.

Attribute #2: The Beginner Must Be Outside of Time (Eternal)

Time was created with the universe, so the Beginner, who created time, must have existed before time "started." This means the Beginner exists in a different dimension than we do. We call that dimension *eternity*. Eternity has no past, no present, no future—it is "outside" of time.

This is difficult for us to grasp, since time is the only reality we know. None of us is eternal. We all had a beginning. But since the Beginner started time, he must have existed before time—he must be eternal.

This agrees with the Bible. Here's only a taste of what it says on God being eternal:

> Abraham planted a tamarisk tree in Beersheba, and there he called on the name of the LORD, *the Eternal God*. (Genesis 21:33)

> Before the mountains were born or you brought forth the whole world, *from everlasting to everlasting* you are God. (Psalm 90:2)

> Your throne was established long ago; you are *from all eternity*. (Psalm 93:2)

> Trust in the LORD forever, for the LORD, the LORD himself, is the Rock *eternal*. (Isaiah 26:4)

> The LORD is the true God; he is the living God, the *eternal King*. (Jeremiah 10:10)

> We declare God's wisdom, a mystery that has been hidden and that God destined for our glory *before time began*. (1 Corinthians 2:7)

The Bible agrees with the Beginner being outside of time—he is eternal.

Attribute #3: The Beginner Must Have Great Power

The Beginner must have unimaginably great power. How could anyone or anything create stars, galaxies, moons, and planets? Who or what could create atoms, energy, time, and space without power far beyond what we can fathom? The Beginner must have power at the highest level. The word for this is *omnipotence*, which means the Beginner must be *all-powerful*.

This too agrees with the Bible, which says the Beginner is all-powerful. Listen to what it says about God's omnipotence:

> Lift up your eyes and look to the heavens: Who created all these? He who brings out the starry host one by one and calls forth each of them by name. Because of his *great power* and mighty strength, not one of them is missing. (Isaiah 40:26)

> With my *great power* and outstretched arm I made the earth and its people and the animals that are on it, and I give it to anyone I please. (Jeremiah 27:5)

> Ah, Sovereign LORD, you have made the heavens and the earth by your great power and outstretched arm. *Nothing is too hard for you.* (Jeremiah 32:17)

> I am the LORD, the God of all mankind. *Is anything too hard for me?* (Jeremiah 32:27)

> With man this is impossible, but with God *all things are possible.* (Matthew 19:26)

Attribute #4: The Beginner Must Be Highly Creative

Have you spent much time thinking about life's amazing diversity? Just look at the world around us. We find mountains, deserts, water, trees, insects, birds, reptiles, amphibians, fish, animals of all kinds and shapes. From delicate butterflies to thundering elephants, life is phenomenally diverse.

Scientists say somewhere between 5 and 30 million different species are alive on earth. There are around three hundred thousand different types of *beetles*, and more species are being discovered each year![1]

What kind of mind could have come up with all these life forms? It certainly is a very, very creative mind—infinitely more creative than we are.

This likewise concurs with the Bible. The biblical God "made all things." Listen to the testimony to his creative capacity:

> God made *two great lights*—the greater light to govern the day and the lesser light to govern the night. He also made the *stars*. (Genesis 1:16)

> God created the great *creatures of the sea* . . . and every winged bird according to its kind. . . . And God said, "Let the land produce *living creatures* . . . that move along the ground, and the wild animals" (Genesis 1:21–24).

> The Lord God made all kinds of *trees* grow out of the ground. (Genesis 2:9)

> The Lord God made a *woman* from the rib he had taken out of the man, and he brought her to the *man*. (Genesis 2:22)

Our list thus far is a solid match for a theistic God. The Beginner cannot have a cause; he must be eternal, omnipotent, and incomparably creative.

We've found some fingerprints of the Beginner, and they're a match for the biblical God.

What Kind of a Designer?

What can we learn *from design* about what the Designer must be like?

Attribute #5: The Designer Must Care About His Creation

Everywhere we look, whether out into the universe or inside a single cell, we find evidence of carefully planned design. We've seen that the universe was designed to support life on earth. Why would Someone or Something design everything with such detail if he didn't care? It certainly seems the Designer does care about what he made.

This agrees with the Bible. Listen to what it says about God's ongoing care and love for his creation.

Give thanks to the LORD Almighty, for the LORD is good; *his love endures forever.* (Jeremiah 33:11)

The LORD is good, a refuge in times of trouble. He *cares* for those who trust in him. (Nahum 1:7)

Cast all your anxiety on him because *he cares for you.* (1 Peter 5:7)

God cares so much about us, he even planned when and where we would live:

From one man he made all the nations, that they should inhabit the whole earth; and he marked out their appointed times in history and the boundaries of their lands. (Acts 17:26)

The Bible tells of God's ultimate care for his creation. It says he loves us so much that he sent Jesus to the cross to die in our place for our sins:

God so *loved* the world that he gave his one and only Son, that whoever believes in him shall not perish but have eternal life. (John 3:16)

God *demonstrates his own love* for us in this: While we were still sinners, Christ died for us. (Romans 5:8)

Attribute #6: The Designer Must Be Supremely Intelligent

The Designer must be more intelligent than anyone or anything we can imagine. He would know and understand everything, for he designed it.

This matches what the Bible says. The biblical God knows even the deepest secrets of our hearts and the most closely guarded thoughts of our minds.

He knows the secrets of the *heart*. (Psalm 44:21)

His *understanding has no limit*. (Psalm 147:5)

Your Father *knows* what you need *before you ask him*. (Matthew 6:8)

Lord, you know everyone's *heart*. (Acts 1:24)

How unsearchable his judgments, and his paths beyond tracing out! (Romans 11:33)

> ## Common Objection: "Given Enough Time, Chance Could Have Produced the Universe"
>
> Here's an example commonly used to try proving this point. Suppose you gave hundreds of monkeys each a keyboard to bang on. Given enough time, isn't there a chance one of them eventually would type a few sequential words? Wouldn't a very, *very* long time increase the chance they'd type a meaningful sentence?
>
> **Answer:** Time doesn't help the chances that a monkey will type a sentence. Chance is nothing, so it cannot help monkeys to type anything, regardless of time involved. A monkey banging on a keyboard produces only chaos. The more time monkeys have, the more *chaos* they'll produce. Adding time to chance does not explain design.
>
> Dropping red, white, and blue confetti from a plane will *never* produce an American flag on your lawn. Taking the aircraft up higher before dropping the confetti yields even less chance of it forming a flag. Time plus chance does not produce complex designs.

Nothing in all creation is hidden from God's sight. (Hebrews 4:13)

God is greater than our hearts, and he *knows everything.* (1 John 3:20)

The Designer cares, and he's supremely intelligent. He is a match for the God of the Bible. We have found more of the Designer's fingerprints.

What Kind of a Moral Lawmaker?

We have seen that there's a universal moral law. What can we learn about what the Moral Lawmaker must be like?

Attribute #7: The Moral Lawmaker Must Have the Authority to Judge, Punish, and Reward All People

There must be a judge for all laws. Someone must have the right or the authority to punish those who break the law; laws would be a farce if we could break them without fear of consequence. The Moral Lawmaker must be able to enforce his laws with all people in all places at all times.

This agrees with the Bible, which claims that God is *the* universal Judge, the only one who can judge all people, everywhere, of all eras.

God is a righteous *judge.* (Psalm 7:11)

He rules the world in righteousness and *judges* the peoples with equity. (Psalm 9:8)

God *judges* people's secrets through Jesus Christ. (Romans 2:16)

The Bible says God will punish all who break his laws.

When the time comes for me to *punish*, I will punish them for their sin. (Exodus 32:34)

I will *punish* the world for its evil, the wicked for their sins. (Isaiah 13:11)

God will remember their wickedness and *punish* them for their sins. (Hosea 9:9)

The Lord knows how to rescue the godly from trials and to hold the unrighteous for *punishment* on the day of judgment. (2 Peter 2:9)

The Bible says Jesus will be the judge of all people.

The Father judges no one, but has entrusted all *judgment* to the Son. (John 5:22)

[Jesus] is the one whom God appointed as *judge* of the living and the dead. (Acts 10:42)

Jesus . . . will *judge* the living and the dead. (2 Timothy 4:1)

The Bible says God will reward all who keep his laws:

You *reward* everyone according to what they have done. (Psalm 62:12)

I the LORD search the heart and examine the mind, to *reward* each person according to their conduct, according to what their deeds deserve. (Jeremiah 17:10)

Your Father, who sees what is done in secret, will *reward* you. (Matthew 6:4)

Look, I [Jesus] am coming soon! My *reward* is with me, and I will give to each person according to what they have done. (Revelation 22:12)

The Bible agrees that only God, as the Moral Lawmaker, has the right to judge, punish, and reward all people.

Attribute #8: The Moral Law Can Be Kept

Any law that's passed must be a law the lawmakers themselves can keep. If we "ought" to do something, then we should be able to do it. Who would pass a law they had no choice but to break? When lawmakers endorse a speed limit, for example, they know drivers can obey it.

In the case of the moral laws, however, we all know that no one on their own can keep them perfectly. We all struggle over and over again. In addition to other failures, we lie, we covet, and we don't always respect our parents. This shows that people cannot be the source of the universal moral law, since no person is morally perfect.

But we've already seen that a Moral Lawmaker (not people) is the moral law's source. *He* must be able to keep it; this would mean he's a perfect being. The Bible says God, the Moral Lawmaker, is in fact morally perfect.

Be perfect, therefore, as *your heavenly Father is perfect.* (Matthew 5:48)

Be holy because *I, the LORD your God, am holy.* (Leviticus 19:2)

God is a *righteous* judge. (Psalm 7:11)

Objection: "Moral Practices Vary From Culture to Culture"

Some say that, for instance, certain cultures don't think it's always wrong to lie. Others believe killing members of opposing tribes is acceptable. So, objectors argue, there isn't actually a universal moral law.

Answer: The moral law isn't what we always *do* but what we know we *ought* to do. It's not how we treat others but how we want to be treated by others. This is universally true, and it's more evidence of a Moral Lawmaker.

We've noted eight "fingerprints" of the Beginner/Designer/ Moral Lawmaker, and they are all a perfect match for the God of the Bible.

The Four Worldviews: What Have the Facts Shown?

We've examined a lot of evidence that shows the existence of an Ultimate Being, or *God*. But the question is, which worldview is a match for this God?

Atheism and the Evidence

Atheism does not match the data. Atheists hold one of two beliefs about the beginning of the universe, both of which are false. Some maintain that the universe has always been here, which is untrue, since we have seen that it had a beginning. Others insist that nothing caused the universe, it just "happened." This cannot be true because *nothing* cannot cause something (or anything).

Neither can atheists explain the design we find throughout the universe. An atheist says no mind is "out there" that could have designed anything. Yet as we've seen, only a Mind can design in a detailed, complex manner such as we see displayed in the universe.

Atheists often appeal to time and chance as design's "cause." But design is not the result of time or chance. No matter how old the earth is, there isn't enough time to account for the development of the incredible design found everywhere. And chance is neither a "thing" *nor* a "cause"— it's merely a mathematical way of explaining how likely (or unlikely) it is that something could happen. Chance cannot cause anything, and it certainly can't explain design.

Some atheists say there is no universal moral law, but they cannot live as though it doesn't exist. They can say they believe there's no moral law, but they don't behave as though it isn't there. They can act contrary to it, but their reaction to having it violated at their expense shows they truly do believe in it.

Atheism cannot explain the beginning of the universe, the design found throughout the universe, or the existence of a universal moral law.

Pantheism and the Evidence

Pantheism doesn't match the facts either.

First, most pantheists believe there's no difference between "god" and nature, maintaining that a godlike force flows through all forms of life and matter. But we've seen that the world had a beginning, and so did all life, so there *is* a difference between the Beginner and all other forms of life and matter. God is the Creator; we are his creation. We are not God. The Designer is not the design any more than the painter is the painting.

Second, pantheists have a problem with the Moral Law-maker. If we're all equally part of god, then who is anyone else to tell me the way to behave? Pantheists can have their own moral code and can even be "good people." If we're all part of god, though, how could one part tell another part what's right and wrong?

Here's what some well-known pantheists have said on the moral law:

Good and evil are one and the same.

Swami Vivekananda[2]

[There is] no difference between the Devil and the Divine.

Bhagwan Shree Rajneesh[3]

I don't believe in morality . . . and I am bent on destroying it. . . . I believe in consciousness, not conscience.

Bhagwan Shree Rajneesh[4]

The Murderer, too, is God.

Vivekananda[5]

Third, pantheists believe we can become God. But we had a beginning; God did not. How can people who had a beginning become the One who never began?

Pantheists believe that they can (by enlightenment) become God. But God has always known he is God. Anyone who suddenly realizes "I am God," isn't God.

Deism and the Evidence

Deists agree that there's a Beginner/Designer/Moral Lawmaker. They believe there's a God. But deists believe that once he created everything, he left the universe on its own; he no longer intervenes or is involved.

As we'll see in chapter 6, if God exists, then miracles are possible. If God can do the miracle of creating the world out of nothing, then certainly he faces no difficulty doing "smaller" miracles. If he can create life to begin with, then it's no problem for him to bring life back to a dead body.

Theism and the Evidence

Theism, which maintains that there's one God who created the universe, is the best match for what we've learned about the Beginner/Designer/Moral Lawmaker. The three primary theistic religions—Judaism, Christianity, and Islam—agree that God created everything, that he designed everything, and that he is the source of the moral law. In the chapters ahead we'll see how Judaism, Christianity, and Islam stand up to the rest of the evidence.

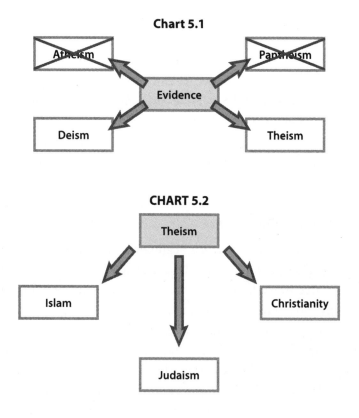

Chart 5.1

CHART 5.2

We've seen the evidence for God's existence and have focused on it because of its importance. Now we're ready to respond to the next challenge: Do miracles really happen?

Miracles

Challenge #4: "Miracles Don't Happen"

Potential problem: Both the Old and New Testaments record many miracles. The four gospels record the greatest miracle claim of all: the resurrection of Jesus Christ. But if in truth there are no miracles, then the Bible is not reliable and Jesus did not rise from the dead.

If you were to take a survey and ask if people believed in miracles, you might be surprised at the results. In a time when many are skeptical about God and Christianity, polls show that most Americans, including many doctors, say they believe in miracles.

What Do We Mean by "Miracle"?

We must start by defining what we mean by a *miracle*. Often we misuse this term, calling a purely unusual event, a simple coincidence, or even an everyday event a miracle. If we stumble and regain our balance we might say, "It's a miracle I didn't break every bone in my body." Or for instance, "It was a miracle I passed that test." So, what is a miracle? Here are three characteristics of a true miracle.

A Miracle Is a Supernatural Intervention

The word *supernatural* means that God is the cause of true miracles. Human power cannot perform a miracle—it's a special act of God. The instant disappearance of a large malignant tumor with no medical help is a miracle. No medical treatment can accomplish this in a moment (or over the span of a few hours, for example). If such a thing happened, it would be because God intervened into the everyday world and healed someone.

A Miracle Transcends (but Doesn't Break) Natural Laws

Suppose a skydiver jumped from a plane at ten thousand feet and his parachute failed to open. The law of gravity would ensure his death upon impact. But suppose that instead, he floated down and gently landed unhurt. Everyone would agree that a miracle had happened.

Yet the law of gravity would not suddenly have been *broken*—it would still be operating as it always has. Instead, gravity would have been *superseded*.

This would be a miracle because God and only God can transcend natural law. He created the law of gravity. He can override it whenever he chooses. A magnet overpowers the law of gravity without breaking it by pulling a scrap of iron upward. A miracle overpowers (without breaking) the laws of nature. It is an *exception* to a natural law.

A Miracle Has a Special Purpose

One day a group of Jews, having seen or heard about the miracles of Jesus, asked him to perform one for them. He responded by calling them "a wicked and adulterous generation" (Matthew 16:4), for they already had enough evidence to know who he was. Jesus did not intend to perform a miracle just to entertain them. *God does not perform miracles merely to amuse or amaze men.*

The main purpose of biblical miracles was to confirm that someone or something truly was from God. Some miracles demonstrated that someone was speaking for God. For example, the miracles for which God empowered Moses were evidence that God had sent him. God said miracles would prove that he was speaking through Moses (for example, see Exodus 3:1–4:9).

God also used miracles to show people that he had sent Jesus. The Gospels record many miracles Jesus did. He turned water into wine, walked on water, fed thousands of people with only a loaf of bread and a few fish, cast out demons, healed diseases and illnesses, and he even raised the dead.

Jesus didn't do these things merely to be nice or to astonish people. He did them to prove who he was: God in the flesh. The apostle John said he recorded Christ's miracles so "that you may believe that Jesus is the Messiah, the Son of God, and that by believing you may have life in his name" (John 20:31). Nicodemus, a ruler of the Jews, said they knew he was from God, since "no one could perform the signs you are doing if God were not with him" (John 3:2).

Miracles likewise were given as proof that the apostles were from God and, therefore, their message was from God as well. Paul wrote that he was given power to perform "signs, wonders and miracles" as *proof* he was God's apostle (2 Corinthians 12:12).

God also used miracles to bring people to Jesus. When Peter raised a dead woman to life (Acts 9:40–42), "many" came to believe in Jesus.

Miracles can be used to teach about who God is. They reveal him to be loving, good, and powerful. When Jesus raised the only son of a widowed mother from the dead, he showed not only God's power but also his love and care for us. When he raised Lazarus, it brought glory to God (John 11:40).

Not Everything Unusual Is a Miracle

Many unusual or remarkable events are not miracles.

First, some unusual incidents happen as a result of natural causes. One such event, widely known as the "Miracle on the Hudson," took place in 2009. Less than two minutes after U.S. Airways flight 1549 had taken off from New York City, headed for Charlotte, its engines collided with large birds and shut down. The pilot in command, Captain Chesley Sullenberger, knowing they couldn't get back to the airport, had no choice but to ditch the plane in the Hudson River. Chances of survival were slim to none.

But "Sully" managed to land the plane on the water, the crew got the passengers out, and all 155 people on board did survive. This event was instantly called a miracle, yet the captain said he didn't think so—rather, it was a case where "everybody did [their] jobs."[1] This doesn't mean God was uninvolved in helping the pilot land the plane successfully; it only means that no natural laws were superseded. A skilled pilot superbly and safely set down the plane under unique and extenuating circumstances.

Second, magic tricks (illusions) are not miracles. A skilled magician can give the *appearance* of having broken a natural law by seeming to make an object materialize out of nowhere, keeping something aloft in the air, or sawing in half and rejoining a person. Sleight-of-hand practitioners guard their secrets, but there's a natural explanation for each one. No illusion breaks a natural law; they're done solely by people and are the result of human acts. (See chart at end of chapter for a comparison of magic and miracles.)

Why Is It So Important Whether Miracles Can Happen?

If there are no miracles, then much of the Old Testament is false. From the time of Moses on down through the prophets, the Old Testament records numerous miracles. If they can't or don't happen, then the Old Testament is not reliable.

Much of the New Testament would be false as well. For starters, it clearly affirms the astonishing miracle of Jesus being born of a virgin. And when John the Baptist sent his disciples to ask Jesus if he was the one they had been waiting for—the one sent from God—he replied:

> Go back and report to John what you have seen and heard: The blind receive sight, the lame walk, those who have leprosy are cleansed, the deaf hear, the dead are raised, and the good news is proclaimed to the poor. (Luke 7:22)

Peter said miracles are proof that Jesus was sent from God:

> Fellow Israelites, listen to this: Jesus of Nazareth was a man accredited by God to you by miracles, wonders and signs, which God did among you through him, as you yourselves know. (Acts 2:22)

If there are no miracles, then Jesus did not rise from the dead. If he was not raised from the dead, then not only are the Gospels false documents but also, as Paul wrote, "If Christ has not been raised, your faith is futile; you are still in your sins" (1 Corinthians 15:17). If miracles do not happen, the Bible is riddled with errors and Christianity is not true.

So, *are* miracles possible?

The answer is simple: *If God exists, miracles are possible.* If there's a God who created and designed the universe, then he can be involved in his creation anytime he chooses. If God is the source of all natural laws, he can supersede them at any time. No creature can tell the Creator that he cannot do what he purposes to do.

A God who could create time, space, stars, planets, moons, and all the variety of life on earth surely could perform more simple acts like healing or helping in a time of need.

This ought to end the debate, but some still raise objections. Here's one of the most common.

Objection: All Religions Claim to Have the Same Kinds of Miracles. Miracles Can't Prove One Belief System to Be True

Suppose the followers of Moses, Buddha, Jesus, Muhammad, Krishna, and Joseph Smith all claimed that their founder walked on water or that he rose from the dead. If such claims were made, and if they were all true, then no one could use them as evidence that only their religion was true.

But are miracle claims truly the same for all faiths? At first, it might seem so. For example, Muhammad is said to have healed the sore eyes of men. Other religious leaders say they can heal via touch or mental powers.

Some Hindus and Buddhists claim they can levitate themselves or others. Joseph Smith said he could translate "reformed Egyptian" even though he couldn't read Egyptian. Mormons claim this showed he was a true prophet of God. Muhammad predicted certain military victories. People involved in the occult claim they can predict the future by looking into crystal balls or by reading cards or tea leaves.

Claims for certain types of miracles, such as visions and special signs, are found in various religions. If they all claimed similar miracles, and if the claims were true, then Jesus' miracles would not prove he was sent from God any more than Joseph Smith was.

Are all the claims alike? Or are biblical miracles different from other miracles?

Six Reasons the Bible's Miracles Are *Not* Like Other Claims

There Are Hundreds of Biblical Miracles

If the biblical books had recorded only a couple of miracles, or a few, it would be tempting to think someone had been inventing stories. By contrast, throughout the Bible, men and women who proved to be reliable, and who claimed to be contemporaries and eyewitnesses of the events, reported dozens upon dozens of miracles.

The Bible records some 250 diverse miracles,[2] sixty in the Gospels alone. And these accounts don't come from people who heard about them from their mother or their grandfather or several generations after the events. They came from men and women who claimed to have *seen* the very miracles of which they bear testimony.

Biblical miracles are unique in their quantity. No other religious source claims so many miracles from actual eyewitnesses.

Biblical Miracles Are Immediate and Permanent

A genuine miracle happens instantly—not over a period of time. When God heals, he heals immediately; all the miracles of Jesus were instantaneous.[3] There are no records of progressive or gradual healings in the Bible.

> Jesus reached out his hand and touched the man. "I am willing," he said. "Be clean!" *Immediately* he was cleansed of his leprosy. (Matthew 8:3)

> Then Jesus said to the centurion, "Go! Let it be done just as you believed it would." And his servant was healed *at that moment*. (Matthew 8:13)

> Peter said . . . "In the name of Jesus Christ of Nazareth, walk." Taking him by the right hand, he helped him up, and *instantly* the man's feet and ankles became strong. (Acts 3:6–7; see also Matthew 9:22; Mark 1:31, 42; John 5:9)

These miracles were all permanent. There were no relapses. No one who was healed became blind or deaf again. Of course, those brought back to physical life ultimately faced physical death once more, as all people must (Romans 5:12; Hebrews 9:27).

Biblical Miracles (Unlike Legends or Fables) Fit Reality

Christian miracles fit into nature, into the world as we know it. The virgin birth was a unique miracle, but once Mary became pregnant, all proceeded normally: She was with child approximately nine months, had a normal delivery, and from all outward appearances, had a normal baby. (Contrary to what Islam claims, Jesus did not speak at birth.)

The miracles of Christ were spectacular, but once he healed someone, their life proceeded normally. None of those he healed became clairvoyant, none could fly, and none retained a halo above his head. There was a miracle, and then everyday life went on as it usually would.

Conversely, non-biblical miracle claims are often bizarre—they *don't* fit the real world. Muhammad claimed he rode to Jerusalem one night on a white-winged horse. Joseph Smith claimed he translated the Book of Mormon into English from a language he did not know, using a magical pair of rose-colored glasses. Tibetan Buddhists claim to have occult powers to suspend people in the air. Nothing like this is found in biblical accounts.

Biblical Miracles Involve No Ritual or Formula

The miracles of the Bible don't follow a prescribed pattern or formula. Jesus healed in a variety of ways. Sometimes the person he healed was present, other times not. Sometimes he touched those he healed; sometimes he didn't. The Bible presents no ritual that someone could or should learn for performing miracles. There are no words to chant, no special touch from a guru or spiritist, and no ceremony to memorize.

Other religions have these elements: secret rituals, for instance, or special rites, and/or magical words and phrases for committing to memory.

Biblical Miracles Were Recorded While Eyewitnesses Were Still Alive

Biblical miracles are based on the records of people who witnessed the events they reported. This is not true of all religions. Miraculous accounts regarding the Buddha came along many years after him. Only a handful of miracle claims for Muhammad are mentioned in the Qur'an, and they are disputed as being fanciful, vague, or lacking the qualities of the truly miraculous. Most of Muhammad's miracle claims weren't even recorded until about 150 years after his death. *None* were recorded by a contemporary eyewitness.[4]

Christianity Makes Unique Miracle Claims for Its Founder

Christianity claims at least three totally unique miracles for Jesus.

First, we have no contemporary documents of any other religious leader or his immediate followers claiming to be virgin-born.

Second, men like Muhammad, Buddha, and Joseph Smith never claimed to be sinless. And as much as their immediate followers revered them, they did not claim they were perfect.

Third, no other religion has claimed their founder rose from the dead. The bodies of Buddha, Krishna, Muhammad, Smith, and the rest are in their graves.

All religions don't *make the same or similar miracle claims.* The biblical miracles are unique and so can be used as evidence that Christianity is true.

What We've Learned

The answer to the allegation that miracles do not or cannot happen is simple: If God exists, then miracles are possible. Because God created everything, including natural laws, he is the Natural Lawmaker, who has the prerogative to temporarily supersede (make exception to) his laws.

Another way to answer this challenge is to say, "If there's a God who can perform special acts, then there can be special acts of God." We know that God can so act because, for instance, he acted this way when he created the world. Men cannot lock God out of his universe. C. S. Lewis said:

> If we admit God, must we admit Miracle? Indeed, indeed, you have no security against it. That is the bargain.[5]

To disprove miracles, we'd first have to disprove God. No one has ever succeeded in doing so. Indeed, few atheists are bold enough to claim that they can actually *disprove* God's existence.

A Comparison Between Miracles and Magic

Miracles	Magic
Under God's control	Under man's control
Done at God's will and in his time	Done at man's will and time
No deception involved	Involves deception
Unusual, but not weird or odd	Unusual and can be odd
Fits into nature	Does not fit into nature
Associated with good	Can be associated with evil
Brings glory to God	Brings glory to man
Used to confirm God's message	Used to entertain or deceive

A Comparison Between Natural Laws and Miracles

Natural Laws	Miracles
Normal. Happens every day	Unusual. Rarely happens
Natural causes	Supernatural cause
Predictable	Unpredictable
Probable	Improbable

Natural Laws	Miracles
No special purpose or message	Special purpose, message
Does not change	God can override, supersede

What About Deism?

In our last chapter we ruled out the worldviews of atheism and pantheism because our evidence did not support their basic beliefs. Now we need to ask how well deism stands up to the evidence. We have seen it denies miracles. But this presents some problems. Why would God create and design everything with such care and then abandon it? Why would God make the universe, and life itself, and then walk away? The deist has no satisfactory answer.

Another problem for deism is that the Designer seems to be concerned about our well-being. As evidence that he loves

(Pantheism also denies miracles, for pantheists hold that one godlike force runs through everything and everyone. If *all* is "god," then there's no supernatural realm beyond the world and thus no supernatural intervention in it.)

Chart 6.1

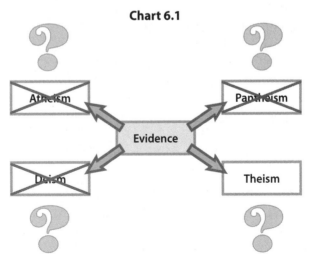

and cares for us, he has fashioned a universe that supports human life. He has given us air to breathe, water to drink, and food to eat. If he cared so much to design the whole universe so human life could thrive, why should we conclude that he doesn't care? Why would that all suddenly change? Again, the deist has no fitting or satisfactory response.

So if there is a God, there can be miracles. No one can tell the Creator he can't intervene in his own creation. At this point, we must rule out deism.

Down to One Worldview: Theism

There are three theistic religions: Judaism, Christianity, and Islam. They all believe in a God who created and designed everything that exists. They all believe in a universal moral law. And they all accept that miracles are possible.

However, Islam has its own problems regarding miracles. Again, Islamic miracle claims for Muhammad were not recorded by eyewitnesses and don't show up until many years after his death.

Muhammad's supposed miracles were reported by someone we'll call Person One, who was quoting another person, whom we'll call Person Two. Person Two was quoting Person Three and so on back for at least a century and a half. Not one miracle claim for Muhammad was noted by an eyewitness.

Also, many of Islam's miracle claims don't match to reality. Muhammad was said to have cut the moon in half with his sword. Palm trees supposedly would lean over to shade him when he stopped in the desert. Rocks would speak when he walked by. Allegedly, his food would speak as well.

Many Islamic claims aren't original either. Some simply copy the earlier miracles of Jesus. For example, Muhammad was said to turn water into milk (since Muslims do not drink wine). There are claims that he fed large groups of people by multiplying food. It's a fair question to ask whether these accounts were borrowed from the New Testament and then altered for Muhammad.

The remaining question will be which of the three theistic religions is the best match for the rest of the evidence we will examine.

Chart 6.2

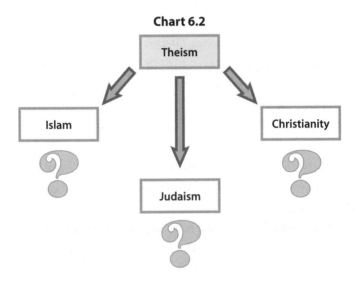

The next challenge we'll examine deals with the New Testament's reliability. Judaism does not recognize it; Islam claims, as do others, that it's been corrupted and is not reliable. What will the evidence show?

7

The New Testament

Challenge #5: "The New Testament's Many Errors Make It Unreliable. It's More Like a Collection of Myths and Legends"

Potential problem: If the New Testament is unreliable, then our beliefs about Jesus—his birth, life, death, and resurrection—have no basis in fact.

For many years, back into the nineteenth and twentieth centuries, various groups of liberal scholars have raised questions about the New Testament's accuracy and reliability. Some of the claims are:

1. The New Testament documents are so far removed from the time of Jesus that we cannot rely on them for accurate information.

2. Myths and legends about Jesus have crept into the gospel accounts.
3. The New Testament is filled with mistakes and contradictions.

Therefore, allegedly, no one can rely on the New Testament as a true or accurate account of anything, especially the life of Christ.

If true, these assertions would mean Christians have put their faith in the wrong person (and in the wrong documents). Unless the New Testament is reliable, we can't claim to be sure of anything about Jesus. We certainly can't claim he died on a cross for our sins and rose from the dead on the third day.

To arrive at an answer to this challenge, we'll ask four key questions:

1. Are the New Testament documents close enough to the recorded events to be reliable?
2. Have the documents been copied correctly?
3. Were the writers reliable? Did they tell the truth?
4. Is there other evidence that shows the New Testament to be reliable?

Question #1: Are the New Testament Documents Close Enough to the Recorded Events to Be Reliable?

Until relatively recently, many critics believed the New Testament documents were written more than a century after the death of Christ. Jesus was crucified about AD 33. This would date the New Testament to about AD 150, by which time eyewitnesses would have been dead and myths and legends would've had time to develop. Therefore, we could not trust the documents.

So our first task is to find out how near to AD 33 the New Testament books were written. The closer to this date, when Jesus lived, the more reliable the documents should be. The farther from that date, the more room there is for claims that the documents are unreliable.

Due to many recent discoveries, as well as technology that helps date ancient documents, we now know approximately when the New Testament was written.

The oldest nearly complete New Testament manuscript, dated to around AD 250, is known as the Chester Beatty Papyri. We have complete books of the New Testament that are dated much earlier, to about AD 200. One is known as the Bodmer Papyri. But this time frame still leaves room for challenges to the New Testament's reliability. However, we can go back further still.

Existing fragments of the New Testament have been dated close to AD 125. One of the earliest, known as the Rylands Library Papyrus, is from the gospel of John. The pieces were found in Egypt; John was living in what is now Turkey when he wrote his gospel, and it would have taken time for it to get from Turkey down to an Egyptian town. Based on this, most scholars now think John's gospel was written sometime in the mid-90s, only about sixty years after Christ's death—when some eyewitnesses to his life, including John, were still alive.

What about Matthew, Mark, and Luke? Many critics now believe their gospels pre-date AD 70. If so, they were written within forty years of Christ's resurrection, when even more eyewitnesses were still alive. One famous critic, Bishop John

Robinson, came to believe some of the Gospels could have been written as early as AD 40.[1]

There are two main reasons any skeptical critic would agree to such an early date.

First, the greatest disaster in Jewish history (to that point) happened in AD 70: the Romans destroyed their nation. Jerusalem was besieged, captured, and crushed. The temple where Jesus had taught was taken apart stone by stone.

If Matthew, Mark, and Luke had been written after AD 70, wouldn't we expect them to at least *refer* to what had happened? This event was cataclysmic and pivotal—and yet they give not even a hint of anything like this befalling them. In fact, the Gospels portray Jerusalem as unharmed and the temple as still standing. Read the following account from Mark:

> As Jesus was leaving the temple, one of his disciples said to him, "Look, Teacher! What massive stones! What magnificent buildings!"
>
> "Do you see all these great buildings?" replied Jesus. "Not one stone here will be left on another; every one will be thrown down" (Mark 13:1–2).

Mark gives the impression that the temple was still right where it had been. Many other references throughout the New Testament present the temple in the same way.

Second, the book of Acts closes with Paul under arrest in Rome around AD 60–62. So it was written about thirty years from Christ's time.

What does this have to do with the dates for Matthew, Mark, and Luke? Well, we know that Luke wrote Acts *after* he wrote his gospel (see Luke 1:1, Acts 1:1–4). If Acts was written around AD 62, then Luke's gospel was written near AD 60 or earlier. Most scholars believe the gospels of Matthew and Mark were written before Luke; this would date them to sometime in the mid-50s.

This is very important, for it means there *wasn't* time for myths and legends about Jesus to develop. Researchers have found that it takes at least two generations (eighty years or more) for their development, because all the eyewitnesses must be dead, along with their children and other people they knew. If less time has elapsed, there are too many people still alive who would challenge anything that has been invented.

For example, take the claim that Jesus rose from the dead. It's the most unlikely claim anyone could ever make. Those who declared it would've been laughed out of Jerusalem unless they had reliable eyewitnesses to back up their words. Eyewitness evidence is exactly what the New Testament writers claimed they had. Many claimed to be eyewitnesses themselves.

- Luke said there were many "*eyewitnesses* and servants of the word" (Luke 1:2).

- Peter and John said there were *eyewitnesses* of Christ's resurrection: "You killed the author of life, but God raised him from the dead. We [Peter and John] are *witnesses* of this" (Acts 3:15).

- Paul said at least 251 other *eyewitnesses* were still alive at the time he wrote 1 Corinthians (around AD 55): "[Jesus] was raised on the third day according to the Scriptures, and . . . he appeared to Cephas [Peter], and then to the Twelve. After that, he appeared to more than five hundred of the brothers and sisters at the same time, *most of whom are still living*" (15:4–6).

Our Conclusion

We find that most of the New Testament was written before AD 70, a reality many skeptics now accept. For instance, William F. Albright, the renowned twentieth-century archaeologist, was highly doubtful about the New Testament's reliability. After studying the evidence for years, though, he determined that "every book of the New Testament was written by a baptized Jew between the 40s and the 80s of the first century AD (very probably sometime between about AD 50 and 75)."[2]

More recently, the noted New Testament scholar Richard Bauckham has demonstrated that its four gospel accounts are based on the eyewitness testimony of those who best knew Jesus.[3] The New Testament documents are close enough to the events they describe to be accurate and reliable.

Question #2: Have the Documents Been Copied Correctly?

Just because the New Testament accounts were recorded in close proximity to Christ's life does not mean they've been copied correctly throughout the subsequent centuries. Many people believe errors have crept into the manuscripts. We must examine the evidence to find whether these documents are, as some allege, filled with mistakes.

We Have a Large Number of Manuscripts

Thousands of New Testament manuscripts have survived. We have around 5,800 partial or complete Greek copies and more than nineteen thousand other copies in different languages.

How does this compare to what survives of other ancient documents? The chart below shows that we have only a few copies of most others.[4]

A Comparison of Ancient Texts

Ancient Author	Title of Work	Total Number of Copies	Time Gap From When Written
Herodotus, Greek historian	History	8	1,350-year gap
Thucydides, Greek historian	History	8	1,300-year gap
Livy, Roman historian	History of Rome	1	1,000-year gap
Tacitus, Roman historian	Annals	20	1,000-year gap
Julius Caesar, Roman historian	Gallic War	10	900+-year gap
Homer, Greek poet	Iliad	c. 500	500-year gap
Various authors	New Testament	Over 5,800 Greek manuscripts alone	100+-year gap to the first gospel

That there are thousands of New Testament copies means we can compare and cross-check all of them to help determine whether the copies are accurate.

How Does Its Time Frame Compare to Other Ancient Sources?

The chart above also shows the long gap between an event's occurrence and its closest related surviving document. Sometimes the gap is more than a thousand years. By comparison, the gap for the New Testament documents is tiny, and once again, it was written when eyewitnesses still lived.

Addressing the Number of "Errors"

In *Misquoting Jesus*, Bart Ehrman (an agnostic critic of the New Testament) has charged that the New Testament copies "differ from one another in so many places that we don't even know how many differences there are."[5] Other sources say the New Testament has as many as 200,000 errors or more. By this accounting, it sounds like the New Testament is so unreliable that we'd be foolish to trust it.

Are such statements true? The answer is *no*, they are not. While there are variants, or "errors," in the copies we have today (not in the originals), the number of variant readings is small. The problem is in how "errors" are counted.

To understand how errors are counted, consider that there is more than one way to spell the name *Ann*. Suppose that, long ago, someone used *Ann* in an original manuscript. Then, as time passed and the next scribe hand-copied the text—remember, for many centuries there was no printing press—he spelled it *Anne*. And then, as additional time went by, suppose 3,000 copies eventually were made based on that change. Would that be one error or 3,000 errors?

The answer is, it would count as 3,000. One miscopied or inserted letter would count as an error every time it was recopied. If you had ten such marks that showed up in 3,000 copies, you'd wind up with 30,000 reported errors.

Of the several "types of errors" claimed for the New Testament, none affects any substantive Christian belief. Here are a few examples of what counts as an error:

- Spelling, grammar, or punctuation that was changed or updated.

- Out-of-date phrases updated or words divided differently.

- A letter or a word that was omitted or was copied twice.

- A letter that was transposed (e.g., *receive* spelled *recieve*).

- Similar letters that were confused. Did Solomon's stables hold 4,000 horses, or 12,000? (See 1 Kings 4:26; 2 Chronicles 9:25.)

- Some texts refer to the "Lord Jesus Christ," others the "Lord Jesus."

- Some texts refer to "the twelve," others "the twelve disciples."

Out of these, not *one* supposed error impacts the meaning of the text or accuracy of a doctrine. While an "error" count of 200,000 sounds significant, upon examination we find this isn't at all the problem some make it out to be.

As it happens, the first edition of Bart Ehrman's book, which reportedly was 100,000 copies, contained at least sixteen errors. If we applied the same method to determine the number of errors, we'd have to say *Misquoting Jesus* contained 1.6 million mistakes, even though not one "error" affected his intended message.

By Comparing the Surviving Manuscripts, We Find That What the Original Said Is Obvious

Usually it's no trouble at all to learn without doubt what the original document said. To illustrate: What if you got any one of these messages?

You have inherited 20 million #ollars.

You have inherited 20 #illion dollars.

Yo# have inherited 20 million dollars.

You have #nherited 20 million dollars.

There's plainly a mistake in each line. Nonetheless, if you got one of these, would you ignore it, or would you go about seeking to collect the money? Of course you'd try to collect it, for regardless of the misprint, you certainly would have gotten the idea—which is that you are suddenly rich!

Because there are so many copies of the New Testament, when an error is found, it's pretty easy to "reconstruct" that exact spot in the original. If each line above was found in one of four different manuscripts, we would know that the original said, "You have inherited 20 million dollars."

With so many hand-rendered copies comes much potential for error. But the sheer number of documents helps us to figure out the correct meaning.

No Christian Belief Has Been Altered

Not one of the so-called errors affects the claims that Jesus is God, was born of a virgin, did miracles, lived a sinless life, died on the cross for our sins, rose from the dead, ascended into heaven, or is coming again.

The New Testament Is More Than 99 Percent Unaffected

Again, with so many manuscripts, we can accurately reconstruct beyond question more than 99 percent of the original text. Various experts, some of them very skeptical, estimate the accuracy of the New Testament—that is, the copies we have right now—at between 98 and 99.9 percent. This means any talk of "errors" is referring to somewhere between one-tenth of a percent and 2 percent of the entire text. And once more, not one mistake has impacted anything essential to the Christian faith.

The renowned Greek scholar A. T. Robertson said, "The real concern is with a thousandth part of the entire text."[6] Accordingly, the reconstructed New Testament text would be 99.9 percent free from any real concern. Church historian Philip Schaff estimated that of the 150,000 variations known in his day, only four hundred (less than three-thousandths of a percent) affected the sense; of those, only fifty were of real significance; and of these, *not one* affected "an article of faith."[7]

How does this compare to other ancient documents? Take a look:

The Accuracy of Ancient Texts

Ancient Text	What Percentage Was Accurately Copied?
The Marabharata, accounts of ancient India	90 percent accurately copied
Iliad of Homer	95 percent accurately copied
The New Testament	99 percent plus accurately copied

While some other texts are very accurate, the New Testament is the most accurate document from the ancient world. If we can't trust it, then we can't trust any ancient account, history book, biography, or *any other* book. Some people choose to believe other accounts but question the New Testament. To say the least, the evidence should make us question that approach.

Our Conclusion: The New Testament Can Be Trusted

Regarding the claim that the New Testament is error-filled, the truth is that it's a highly reliable document we can trust.

Question #3: Were the New Testament Writers Reliable?

The New Testament writers were eyewitnesses, or associates of eyewitnesses, of the events they recorded. Here is some of what they said:

> *The man who saw it* [the crucifixion] has given testimony, and his testimony is true. (John 19:35)

> This is *the disciple who testifies to these things and who wrote them down.* We know that his testimony is true. (John 21:24)

> God has raised this Jesus to life, and *we are all witnesses* of it. (Acts 2:32)

> We cannot help speaking about *what we have seen and heard.* (Acts 4:20)

> We are *witnesses of everything* he did in the country of the Jews and in Jerusalem. They killed him by hanging him on a cross. (Acts 10:39)

> He was not *seen* by all the people, but *by witnesses* whom God had already chosen—by us who ate and drank with him after he rose from the dead. (Acts 10:41)

To the elders among you, I appeal as a fellow elder and *a witness of Christ's sufferings* who also will share in the glory to be revealed. (1 Peter 5:1)

These men claimed to have seen Christ's miracles, death, resurrection, and ascension into heaven.

However, some critics still challenge the New Testament and allege that the writers may have made up these events. In other words, they charge that the writers were not reliable—that they didn't tell the truth.

There are many facts by which we can know that, in contrast, the writers *were* trustworthy and *did* tell the truth. The following are several reasons we can count on their reliability and honesty.

They Include Embarrassing Details About Themselves

Most people who record an account in which they play an important part endeavor to make themselves look as good as possible. No one wants to be embarrassed by what they actually said or did.

Yet the gospel writers look pretty bad. For example, they establish the following facts *about themselves*:

They *failed to understand* what Christ was saying to them about his upcoming death. (See Mark 9:32; Luke 18:34; John 12:16.)

They *fell asleep* in the garden of Gethsemane after Jesus had asked them to stay awake and pray with him. (See Mark 14:37–42.)

They *ran away* like cowards and even denied Jesus following his arrest. (See Matthew 26:55–56.)

Some of them *doubted* that Jesus was raised from the dead. (See Matthew 28:17; Luke 24:11; John 2:18–22; 20:8–9, 24–28.)

They Include Events About Jesus' Burial and Resurrection That They Certainly Would Not Have Invented

Who buried Jesus? Not the disciples. They were in hiding. Who were the first resurrection witnesses? The women, not the men, who followed Jesus.

Christ's followers wouldn't have invented these facts, which, once again, are anything but complimentary. If they'd made up these accounts, they'd have presented themselves as the first witnesses, since in the culture of that day, the testimony of women wasn't accepted as legally valid.

They Include More Than Thirty Historically Confirmed People

The New Testament is filled with the names of people known to have lived at that time. In one text, where he also marks an exact date (AD 29), Luke mentions eight:

> In the fifteenth year of the reign of Tiberius Caesar—when Pontius Pilate was governor of Judea, Herod tetrarch of Galilee, his brother Philip tetrarch of Iturea and Traconitis, and Lysanias tetrarch of Abilene—during the high-priesthood of Annas and Caiaphas, the word of God came to John son of Zechariah in the wilderness. (Luke 3:1–2)

History confirms that these were real men who lived at the time of Jesus. They also were powerful men of high standing who could have caused a lot of trouble for the disciples if their claims about Christ's death and resurrection were false. Lying about these events could have cost them everything.

The Gospel Accounts Aren't All Precisely Alike

If you and some friends determined to make up a story, you'd make sure your accounts agreed with one another. But the gospel writers record some differences about certain events. They don't record contradictions, yet they do explain things from different angles.

Detectives who investigate crimes will tell you that witnesses who lie in order to cover up their roles all try to get their stories to match in minute detail. When investigators hear different witnesses all saying *exactly* the same thing, they immediately become suspicious. In reality, people who see the same incident always report it with some measure of uniqueness, depending on their individual perspectives—where they were standing, what they heard, what they noticed or observed, and so on.

If the disciples were lying about what they recorded, why didn't they first work out all the details to be sure it all precisely "matched"? That they report the same events a bit differently suggests they were telling the truth.

They Don't Exaggerate the Miracles of Jesus

Many of the miracle accounts aren't overly exciting or very imaginative. A blind man sees. A lame man walks. That's *all*? Why not include more phenomenal details—say, Jesus turning his arms into wings and instantly traversing vast distances (or soaring on a white horse)? Think about it: If you were going to invent miracle claims, what kinds of details would you insert?

The Men Who Wrote the Gospels Did Not Deny Their Testimony Under Persecution or in the Face of Death

People lie about a variety of things for a variety of reasons. But if they suddenly face hard times or even a death sentence, sooner or later someone starts telling the truth. No one wants to die for a lie they invented.

The historical record shows that every one of the apostles suffered profoundly for his belief that Jesus died, was buried, and rose again on the third day. All but John were martyred and suffered gruesome deaths.

Yet none ever changed his account of the life, death, and resurrection of Jesus. Why? The only reasonable answer is that they were telling the truth. They had nothing to gain by continuing to lie. No one was getting rich off of carefully contrived lies. No one got a book deal or a film contract. All they got was more persecution, hardship, suffering, and eventually, agonizing death.

Thus, we must ask: What happened two thousand years ago that so radically changed these frightened men who'd been huddled in fear behind locked doors? What turned them into the fearless evangelists who marched onto the temple grounds, took the gospel to the empire, and held to their testimony even as they were beaten, burned, tortured, and killed? The only explanation is that they saw the risen Lord and were holding to the truth.

Using the "Rules of Evidence" to Determine the Truth of the Eyewitness Testimony

Dr. Simon Greenleaf, a founder of Harvard Law School, developed what became known as the "Rules of Evidence"—the rules that determine what kind of testimony, exhibits, and information will be admitted into evidence in a court of law.

Greenleaf was a highly respected professor and attorney, but he was not a Christian. In fact, he was skeptical of Christianity and often would make fun of believers in his class. One day a group of Christian students challenged him to take his own standards for courtroom evidence and apply it to the claim that Jesus rose from the dead. He agreed to the challenge, certain he would prove the resurrection accounts to be false.

Instead, he was shocked by his own results. He was convinced the New Testament accounts were reliable, and he became a believer. He concluded that the writers were telling the truth for several reasons.

These were Greenleaf's own standards for a witness:

ARE THE WITNESSES HONEST? ARE THEY TELLING THE TRUTH?[8]

Simon Greenleaf found that the men who wrote the New Testament had high moral standards. They told others not to lie. They warned people not to become drunk, not to commit adultery. They exhorted everyone to love others, be humble, take care of orphans and widows, pursue righteousness (e.g., see Romans 12:10; Colossians 3:9; 1 Timothy 3:8; 2 Timothy 2:22; Titus 3:2; Hebrews 13:4; James 1:27).

Greenleaf concluded that these were honest men who had told the truth about the resurrection of Jesus Christ. He later wrote:

> It is incredible that bad men should invent falsehoods to promote the religion of the God of truth. . . .[9]
>
> Either [the apostles] were . . . [more skilled] in the arts of deception than all others, before or after them, or they have truly stated the astonishing things which they saw and heard.[10]

ARE THE WITNESSES BELIEVABLE?[11]

Greenleaf found that the authors were all of at least normal intelligence. Their writings are not the rants of unstable men. The apostle Paul, who wrote most of the New Testament books, was highly educated. Luke, a doctor, independently investigated the facts for himself. Greenleaf concluded that the New Testament was written by believable witnesses.

ARE THERE ENOUGH WITNESSES?[12]

An attorney always hopes to have more than one witness to testify. With one, the case may not be very strong. Two or more eyewitnesses are preferable.

Greenleaf noted that several different men wrote the New Testament. Five authors—Matthew, John, Peter, Paul, and James—were themselves eyewitnesses to the resurrection. Luke interviewed eyewitnesses. No other event from the ancient world had this many witnesses all stating the same essential facts. Greenleaf concluded that there were sufficient witnesses.

ARE THE WITNESSES CONSISTENT?[13]

Witnesses should be consistent on all the primary facts. At the same time, as they always see things from their own point of view, we should expect some secondary details to have a degree of difference.

Greenleaf found that the writers agreed on all the main points. They all agreed that Jesus rose from the dead, yet each told the story in his own way. His conclusion: These men were consistent in all the basic areas while providing details from their individual vantage point. They were telling the truth.

Question #4: Is There Other Evidence That Shows the New Testament to Be Reliable?

The answer to this, our last question, is yes—there is outside (extrinsic) evidence that shows the New Testament to be reliable. Let's look at five areas.

History Confirms the New Testament's Reliability

The entire Bible is filled with historical names, places, and events. It covers a period of more than four thousand years. It's a record of actual empires, nations, and rulers. The Old Testament mentions historical groups of people (such as the Canaanites, Hittites, Moabites, and Philistines). The New Testament accurately details the names and titles of various people in the Roman Empire and the Jewish nation. It accurately records the location of cities and ports as well as the distances and travel time between them. It includes data about the customs, politics, even the food and clothing of its time. The Bible has proven to be historically accurate in all these areas.[14]

Jewish Rabbis Confirm the New Testament's Reliability

Most Jewish rabbis did not believe Jesus was the Messiah. They did not believe he rose from the dead. Yet they recorded the following historical facts about him:

- He was from Nazareth.
- He was hanged (crucified) on the eve of Passover for heresy (claiming to be God) and for misleading people.
- His disciples healed the sick in his name.[15]

Josephus Confirms the New Testament's Reliability

Moreover, the famous Jewish historian and contemporary of Jesus, Flavius Josephus, wrote of "the brother of Jesus, the so-called Christ, whose name was James . . ." (*Antiquities* XX 9:1). And in a more explicit passage in the *Antiquities,* he says: "At this time there was a wise man who was called Jesus. . . . Pilate ordered Him to be condemned and to die. And those who had become His disciples did not abandon His discipleship. They reported that He had appeared to them three days after His crucifixion and that He was alive" (XVIII.33, Arabic text).

A non-Christian historian recorded the death and resurrection of Jesus Christ.

Tacitus and Thallus Confirm the New Testament's Reliability

Together, Tacitus and Thallus, two Roman historians, recorded that Jesus was executed by Pontius Pilate in the time of the emperor Tiberius. They also chronicled the following events at the time Christ died:

On the whole world there pressed a most fearful darkness; and the rocks were rent by an earthquake, and many places in Judea and other districts were thrown down.[16] (See also Matthew 27:52; Mark 15:33; Luke 23:44.)

The accounts of historians and religious leaders, Jewish and Gentile, support the New Testament accounts of the life of Jesus. Indeed, altogether they record these facts:

1. He was from Nazareth.
2. He lived a virtuous life.
3. He performed unusual feats.
4. He introduced new teaching.
5. He was crucified under Pontius Pilate.
6. His disciples believed he rose from the dead.
7. His disciples denied polytheism.
8. His disciples worshiped him.
9. His teachings and disciples spread rapidly.
10. His followers believed they were immortal.
11. His followers had contempt for death.
12. His followers renounced material goods.[17]

Archaeology Confirms the New Testament's Reliability

For more than two centuries, archaeology has been proving again and again that the Bible is historically reliable. Here are just a few examples of archaeological support for the New Testament accounts:

- The synagogue in Capernaum where Christ taught has been found. (Mark 1:21: "They went to Capernaum, and when the Sabbath came, Jesus went into the synagogue and began to teach.")

- Peter's home in Capernaum has been found. (Matthew 8:14: "When Jesus came into Peter's house, he saw Peter's mother-in-law lying in bed with a fever.")

- The Pools of Siloam and Bethesda have been found in the old city of Jerusalem. They're in the exact places and match the exact descriptions found in the New Testament. (John 9:11: "The man they call Jesus made some mud and put it on my eyes. He told me to go to Siloam and wash. So I went and washed, and then I could see." John 5:2: "There is in Jerusalem near the Sheep Gate a pool, which in Aramaic is called Bethesda and which is surrounded by five covered colonnades.")

- Proof of Pilate's existence has been found. A large limestone block near the Roman amphitheater in Caesarea, Israel, bears a message that says it's from "Pontius Pilate, Prefect of Judea." Coins found and dated from AD 29–31 bear the name Pontius Pilate.

- Evidence has been found of men who were crucified in the same manner as described in the gospel accounts. An ancient burial suite uncovered in Jerusalem in 1968 contained thirty-five bodies. The heel bones of one skeleton had a seven-inch nail that had been driven through both feet. Small pieces of a wooden board were still attached to one end. Spikes had been driven between the arm bones, and the legs had been broken below the knee. These bones, dated to the time of Christ, match the type of crucifixion described in the Gospels.[18]

Archaeology has provided us with one reason after another to accept the New Testament documents. The archaeologist Nelson Glueck wrote:

> It may be stated categorically that no archaeological discovery has ever controverted a biblical reference. Scores of archaeological findings have been made which confirm in clear outline or exact detail historical statements in the Bible.[19]

Objection #1: There are many apparent contradictions in the New Testament

Here are two examples of alleged contradictions:

Example #1: The death of Judas. Matthew 27:5 says he "hanged himself." Acts 1:18 says he "fell headlong, his body burst open and all his intestines spilled out."

Answer: Judas hanged himself on a tree. Later, when the rope broke, his body fell from the tree and burst open. The rope may have broken when someone tried to cut down the body; it may have broken naturally; there are several possibilities. It does not pose a contradiction.

Example #2: The number of angels at the tomb of Jesus. Matthew 28:5 refers to one. John 20:12 says Mary saw two.

Answer: Matthew doesn't say there was only one angel—he only refers to one, and whenever there are two, there is always one.

That there are difficult passages in Scripture should not cause us to conclude that the Bible is wrong. Whatever the problem is, it is with us—we've not yet understood the possible solutions or grasped what's actually being said. The more we study the Bible and the evidence for it, the more we eliminate claims of contradictions.

Objection #2: No one could remember such long parts of Scripture as the Sermon on the Mount. Therefore, the New Testament is not a reliable record of what Jesus really said and did.

Answer: Actually, at that time, many men *were* trained to memorize historical accounts and lengthy stories. Matthew, a tax collector who kept detailed records, could easily have recorded Jesus' words. Luke, a doctor, tells us he researched events carefully and interviewed eyewitnesses.

Many people today have memorized entire books of the Bible. In some places, like China, Christians memorize long passages and recite them to others, since so many don't have a complete Bible.

There is also evidence that they kept written records of what Jesus said (Matthew 13:52).

Jesus himself promised that his Spirit would come and teach the disciples "all things" and would remind them of everything Jesus said to them (John 14:26).

Why do many professors and scholars reject the New Testament documents if there's so much evidence in their favor?

There's enormous academic pressure in colleges and universities to support certain points of view. Promotions, power, respect, even job security can be at stake. If you're "too Christian" or "too religious," you may not get your books published or receive tenure. (See the film *Expelled: No Intelligence Allowed!* if you don't believe this.)

Also, most professors and teachers today are naturalists. Worldviews are not easily changed. People are affected by pride. Sometimes evidence is rejected because minds are already made up, closed to other points of view.

What We've Learned

As to the claim that the New Testament is filled with errors, we have found the opposite to be true. It's an accurate, reliable document we can trust.

1. It was written within the eyewitnesses' lifetime. Not enough time went by for the invention of myths or legends; its time frame is reliable.
2. The documents have been well copied. The New Testament is more than 99 percent error-free; no error affects any basic Christian belief.
3. The writers were reliable. The New Testament accounts are based on the eyewitness testimony of honest men.
4. The New Testament has been repeatedly confirmed by outside sources.

There is far more solid evidence for the New Testament than for any other ancient document. No other ancient account has more manuscripts to check and compare. No other has been more accurately copied.

So when the New Testament says Jesus said something, we can know he actually said it. When the New Testament says Jesus did something, we can know he actually did it. His life, death, and resurrection is not just a good story. It *happened*! It's not merely a movie or a book. It's *historical*! It's *true*.

Now that we know we can rely on the New Testament, we'll turn to challenges that focus on Jesus. The first objection we'll examine: Was Jesus really God? Did he claim to be God? What's the evidence? Let's check it out.

8

Is Jesus God? (Part I)

Challenge #6: "Jesus Never Claimed to Be God"

Potential problem: If Jesus never claimed to be God, why would we think he is God?

People have a lot of different ideas about Jesus. Some say they think he was a good man, or a wise teacher. Some claim they want to follow his moral teachings, but not everyone thinks he is God.

Others say Jesus never even claimed to be God. They argue that you won't find one place in the New Testament where he came right out and said, "I'm God!" If Jesus *is* God, it'd be a bit odd for him never to have said so. Why would he come to earth and not tell anyone who he truly is?

So is this true? Did Jesus ever flat-out say he is God?

Evidence That Jesus Claimed to Be God

Jesus Claimed to Be the Great "I AM" of Exodus 3:14

In the Old Testament, the one word or one name that identified the God of Israel can be translated "I AM." Jewish scribes wrote it out in four letters, *YHWH*, and today most pronounce it as *Yahweh* (some as "Jehovah"). This name is often written out in our Old Testament as "LORD" (all caps) and is cited in many other books (like this one) as "LORD" (small caps) to set it apart from other words that also mean "Lord" or "lord."

The origins are found in Exodus. When Moses asked God his name, God said to Moses,

> I AM WHO I AM. This is what you are to say to the Israelites: "I AM has sent me to you.". . . . Say to the Israelites, "The LORD [*YHWH*], the God of your fathers—the God of Abraham, the God of Isaac and the God of Jacob—has sent me to you. This is my name forever, the name you shall call me from generation to generation" (3:14–15).[1]

God gave this name to his people to identify himself and to separate himself from all other so-called gods. To a Jew, it applied only to God—it was his unique name. The scribes who copied "the Name" considered it so sacred that when writing, they would perform a special ceremony before recording it. This name was so special that only the High Priest could speak it, and only in the temple in Jerusalem. *This was the holy name for the one true God.*

What does this have to do with Jesus? Regarding the objection that he never "directly claimed to be God," Jesus applied *this* word, a word Jews would not even speak, God's most holy name—"*the Name*"—to himself. Here are two examples that show Jesus doing this.

First, when the Jews accused Jesus of being demon-possessed, he said that he was not, and went on to say that he was greater than Abraham: "Your father Abraham rejoiced at the thought of seeing my day; he saw it and was glad" (John 8:56).

The Jews could not believe what they'd just heard: "'You are not yet fifty years old,' they said to him, 'and you have seen Abraham!'" (8:57). Then Jesus stunned them with his reply: "Very truly I tell you . . . before Abraham was born, *I am*!" (8:58).

The Jews knew *exactly* what he meant—there was no doubt whatsoever that he was claiming to be God. They picked up stones to kill him, which they'd do again when he said, "I and the Father are one" (John 10:30). They intended to stone him "for blasphemy, because you, a mere man, *claim to be God*" (v. 33).

Second, Jesus also boldly used "the Name" to claim his divine identity on the night he was betrayed by Judas. Read John's account carefully, and note that the word *he,* in parentheses, is not in the original text. We've emphasized where he used the term *YHWH* ("I AM").

Judas came to the garden, guiding a detachment of [Roman] soldiers and some [Jewish] officials from the chief priests and the Pharisees. They were carrying torches, lanterns and weapons.

Jesus, knowing all that was going to happen to him, went out and asked them, "Who is it you want?"

"Jesus of Nazareth," they replied.

"*I* AM (~~he~~)," Jesus said. (And Judas the traitor was standing there with them.) When Jesus said, "*I* AM (~~he~~)," they drew back and fell to the ground.

Again he asked them, "Who is it you want?"

"Jesus of Nazareth," they said.

"I told you that *I* AM (~~he~~)" (John 18:3–8).

Jesus had once again applied the sacred name to himself. And did you notice the effect it had? When he said it, "they drew back and fell to the ground" (18:6).

Try to envision the scene. Jesus was unarmed. Except for the one sword Peter had, the small group of disciples was unarmed too. Yet Jesus' speaking God's holy name and claiming it for himself carried such power that in the face of it, trained, armed soldiers couldn't remain standing.[2]

Anyone who says "Jesus never came right out and said he was God" does not understand how to think like the Jews of Jesus' day! Once again: *They* had absolutely no doubts about what he meant. His claims to be God were so clear and direct that they sought to execute him.

Jesus Claimed and Used the Titles of God

Names of God, Claims of Jesus

God Is Called ...	Jesus Claimed to Be ...
Lord: Psalm 110:1	Lord: Mark 2:28
King: Psalm 5:2; 29:10	King: John 18:36–37
Shepherd: Genesis 49:24	Shepherd: Matthew 2:6; John 10:11
Light: Psalm 27:1	Light: John 1:1–5; 8:12; 9:5
Living Water: Jeremiah 2:13	Living Water: John 4:11–14; 7:38

In using these titles, Jesus was plainly telling his people he was God in the flesh. They knew it, didn't believe him, and tried to kill him for it.

Jesus Accepted the Worship and Honor Due to God Alone

The Bible is clear: *Only* God is to be worshiped. And all Jews knew this. They were told over and over to worship God alone, as Jesus himself also said: "It is written: 'Worship the Lord your God, and serve him only'" (Matthew 4:10). However, on at least ten different occasions he accepted worship from people.

Men healed of leprosy, of demon-possession, and of blindness all worshiped Jesus (e.g., Matthew 8:2; Mark 5:6; John 9:38). He accepted worship from his disciples (Matthew 14:33; 28:17; John 20:28) as well as from Jewish and non-Jewish women (Matthew 15:25; 20:20; 28:9). In fact, he never *refused* worship from *anyone*. In accepting worship, Jesus was clearly claiming to be God.

Jesus Commanded His Disciples to Pray in His Name

Jews were to pray to God and to God alone. Yet Jesus told his followers to pray to *him*! He said they could ask him "for anything in my name, and I will do it" (John 14:14). Not only was he saying to pray to him, and to ask in his name, he also was claiming he could and would answer prayer. Any Jew knew: Only God can do this. Jesus' command was an obvious claim to be God.

Jesus Claimed to (and Did) Lead a Sinless Life

Jesus set the pinnacle of moral standards. He said we're to love our enemies. We're to do good to all, even to those who hate us. We're to pray for those who treat us wrongly. We're to feed and clothe those less fortunate. We're to turn the other cheek if someone hurts us. We're not to retaliate or strike back. You cannot find a higher standard than the one Jesus set in directing us to love God with all our heart, soul, strength, and mind and to love others as much as we love ourselves.

But Jesus didn't just tell us to live like this—he also set the very example we're to follow, by living a perfect life. No other religious leader ever claimed to be perfect. Muhammad asked for forgiveness (Qur'an 47:19). Siddhartha Gautama (Buddha) deserted his wife. Joseph Smith practiced polygamy (over his first wife's objections). The Bible's great heroes had many moral failures.

Everyone but Jesus. There was no moral failure on his part. He pointed this out to the Jews one day, saying, "Can any of you prove me guilty of sin?" (John 8:46). No one responded. By claiming to lead a sinless life, Jesus was in effect claiming to be God.

Those who best knew him concurred:

We have one who has been tempted in every way, just as we are—yet he did not sin. (Hebrews 4:15)

[Christ is] a lamb without blemish or defect. (1 Peter 1:19)

He committed no sin, and no deceit was found in his mouth. (1 Peter 2:22)

Christ also suffered once for sins, the righteous for the unrighteous. (1 Peter 3:18)

He is righteous. (1 John 2:29)

He is pure. (1 John 3:3)

God made him who had no sin to be sin for us. (2 Corinthians 5:21)

[He] is holy, blameless, pure, set apart from sinners. (Hebrews 7:26)

Christ . . . offered himself unblemished to God. (Hebrews 9:14)

Even his enemies agreed:

Judas: "I have sinned . . . for I have betrayed innocent blood" (Matthew 27:4).

Pilate: "I find no basis for a charge against this man" (Luke 23:4).

Pilate's wife: "Don't have anything to do with that innocent man" (Matthew 27:19).

Centurion: "Surely this was a righteous man" (Luke 23:47). "Surely he was the Son of God!" (Matthew 27:54).

Thief on the cross: "This man has done nothing wrong" (Luke 23:41).

The Herodians: "Teacher . . . we know that you are a man of integrity and that you teach the way of God in accordance with the truth. You aren't swayed by others, because you pay no attention to who they are" (Matthew 22:16).

The testimony of friend and foe confirm what Jesus said, and showed, about his own character. His deity is the best explanation for his being without sin.

Jesus Claimed to Do What Only God Can Do

Only God has power and authority to forgive sins, act as ultimate judge, and determine each person's final destiny. Jesus claimed the prerogative for all these as well (e.g., see Mark 2:7–10; Matthew 25:31–32; John 5:24), and thereby was claiming he is God.

Jesus Claimed (and Proved) to Have Power Only God Has

If Jesus is God, he should be able to do anything God has power to do.

The Power of God—The Power of Jesus

Only God Has Power . . .	Jesus . . .
To do miraculous healings	Healed a wide variety of diseases. He healed the blind, the lame, the lepers, the deaf, and the dumb. (Luke 7:20–22)
To accurately predict the future (Isaiah 37:26; 48:3)	Accurately predicted the future (Matthew 24:1–2)
Over nature	Walked on water, calmed storms. The wind obeyed him; he turned water into wine; he multiplied bread.
Over demons and Satan	Cast out demons; rebuked Satan (Mark 1:39; Matthew 4:10)
Over death	Raised the dead. (Matthew 9:18–26; John 11:43–44)

When Jesus showed he had the power of God, he was confirming he *is* God.

Jesus Claimed Other Titles That the Jews Applied Only to God

Again, one of the reasons people say Jesus didn't claim to be God is they don't know how to think like first-century Jews—*they* had no doubt about whom Jesus said he was. So we have to think like they did.

Jesus applied two *unique* titles to himself, and the Jews of his time understood each to be a clear statement of his divinity.

TITLE #1: SON OF GOD

Jesus said he was the Son of God:

> Why then do you accuse me of blasphemy because I said, "I am God's Son?" (John 10:36).

Jesus did not mean he is the Son of God in some biological sense—his claim is equality with God. In Greek, the original language, "Son of" can also mean "the same as" or "equal to." Jesus was saying he is "God's equal."

The Jews plainly understood his claim to deity when he applied this term to himself. Speaking to Pilate about why Jesus should be put to death, "The Jewish leaders insisted, 'We have a law, and according to that law he must die, because he claimed to be the Son of God'" (John 19:7).

In addition to calling himself the Son of God, Jesus also called God "my Father." To the Jews, this was another claim to *be* God. No Jew in his right mind would have called God "*my* Father."

> "Why were you searching for me?" he asked. "Didn't you know I had to be in *my Father's* house?" (Luke 2:49).

To those who sold doves he said, "Get these out of here! Stop turning *my Father's* house into a market!" (John 2:16).

Very truly I tell you, it is not Moses who has given you the bread from heaven, but it is *my Father* who gives you the true bread from heaven. (John 6:32)

The Jews knew what Jesus was claiming. In response, as we have seen, they turned against him and sought to kill him.

For this reason [the Jews] tried all the more to kill him; not only was he breaking the Sabbath, but *he was even calling God his own Father, making himself equal with God.* (John 5:18)

TITLE #2: SON OF MAN

Jesus used "Son of Man," his favorite title for himself, repeatedly throughout the Gospels. Some people think this means that Jesus was the son of a man—a man named Joseph. But that's not what this meant to a Jew.

When Jesus used this term, he was not referring to being a man or to being the son of a man. Jesus was referencing a divine person Daniel wrote about in the Old Testament, a unique person who would come in the future:

In my vision at night I looked, and there before me was one *like a son of man*, coming with the clouds of heaven. . . . He was given *authority, glory* and sovereign *power;* all nations and peoples of every language *worshiped* him. His dominion is an *everlasting* dominion that will not pass away, and his *kingdom* is one that will never be destroyed. (Daniel 7:13–14)

This man whom Daniel foretold would be worshiped and would have authority, glory, and power. To whom does glory belong but God? Who is worthy of worship but God? Who but God has authority over all?

This man also would have a kingdom that will never pass away or be destroyed. Whose kingdom will last forever, except God's?

When Jesus applied this title to himself, the Jews understood that he was not claiming he was Joseph's son; he was claiming to be *this* divine figure.

And we can see this plainly. The night Jesus was arrested—the night before he was crucified—he was on trial before the Jewish authorities:

> The high priest asked him, "Are you the Messiah, the Son of the Blessed One?"
>
> "I am," said Jesus. "And you will see the *Son of Man* sitting at the right hand of the Mighty One and coming on the clouds of heaven."
>
> The high priest tore his clothes. "Why do we need any more witnesses?" he asked. "You have heard the *blasphemy*. What do you think?"
>
> They all condemned him as worthy of death. (Mark 14:61–64)

When Jesus used the term *Son of Man,* Caiaphas and everyone else in the room knew he was referring to Daniel's prophecy and claiming equality with God; he even said they would see him coming "on the clouds of heaven," as Daniel described. That night they *all* grasped what he was saying. Jesus was saying he was God's equal.

And so the high priest tore his garments. According to custom, whenever anyone committed blasphemy, the person sitting in judgment was to stand and rend his robes so severely that they could never be mended. This was a symbol to mark how seriously the Jews treated the crime.[3]

Jesus used this term again and again to tell them who he was. They rightly understood it as a clear claim to have God's glory, power, and authority, to be worthy of worship, and to possess the everlasting kingdom.

Remember: To fathom the degree to which Jesus claimed to be God, we have to think like the people to whom he was speaking.

Three Choices: Is Jesus a Lunatic, a Liar, or the Lord?

Jesus' claim to be God is so clear in the Gospels that C. S. Lewis put it in no uncertain terms, saying that Jesus must be one of the following:

1. Jesus was a lunatic. He thought he was God, but he wasn't. Therefore, he was crazy, like someone who thinks he's Napoleon Bonaparte.
2. Jesus was a liar. Jesus said he was God, but he knew he wasn't.
3. Jesus is Lord (God).[4]

Lewis was saying we have to make a choice. Jesus is one of these three: a lunatic, a liar, or the Lord. Which one best fits the evidence?

First, Jesus was not a lunatic. He was in touch with reality; he did not experience hallucinations; he did not hear "voices"; he did not see bizarre visions. He related well to a wide variety of people, rich and poor, young and old; he formed, fostered, and sustained lasting relationships with those closest to him; and he changed the lives of those around him. Even contemporary skeptics admire his ethical teaching. *Lunatic* doesn't fit the facts.

Second, Jesus was not a liar. Even his enemies considered him a moral man. He taught the highest of moral laws, and he lived up to the highest of moral standards. Those who knew him best could not accuse him. Even his enemies acknowledged he was without fault. *Liar* doesn't fit the facts.

Jesus is Lord. It's the only remaining choice.

Think about Jesus this way: If God became a man, what would he be like? What would he do? Here's a list of what we could expect to happen if God came to earth as a man. Compare it to what happened in the life of Jesus!

If God Came, What Would We Expect?

We Would . . .	What Happened in Jesus' Life:
expect him to have a different entrance into life.*	He was virgin-born; angels appeared; there were signs in the sky.
expect him to tell people that he was God.	Jesus clearly told men he was God.
expect him to live a perfect life.	Jesus was without sin.
expect him to provide evidence he was God.	Jesus performed miracles, had power over nature, cast out demons.
expect him to have power over disease and death.*	Jesus healed men and women, raised the dead.
expect him to speak the greatest words ever spoken.*	Jesus taught the greatest moral commands of any man. Men said, "No one ever spoke the way this man does" (John 7:46).
expect him to provide a means by which men could come to know him. (Why would God come and not have us know him and why he came?)	Jesus provided a way for us to know him; he said he was the way to God.

We Would . . .	What Happened in Jesus' Life:
expect him to have a lasting and universal influence.*	Jesus has influenced the lives of more men and women than any other man in history.
expect him to have a message that would speak to all men and women, at all times, in all places.	The gospel of Jesus Christ has reached men and women in every place, in every generation.
expect him to relate to men and women in the various parts of society and culture.	Jesus related to the rich, poor, young, old, Jews, and Gentiles.
expect him to change the lives of those who met him and knew him.	Jesus changed the lives of those he met, and the lives of those he knew.
expect him to satisfy the spiritual hunger of men and women.*	Jesus has satisfied the spiritual needs of men and women; he is the Bread of Life; the Living Water.
expect him to show sympathy for our problems, sickness, and pain.	Jesus showed great empathy for the physical and spiritual needs of men.
expect him to provide some kind of solution to sin, pain, and suffering.	Jesus died for our sins, and comforts us when we suffer, have pain, and face problems.
expect him to leave some kind of permanent record that he was here. (Why would God come and not leave a record for others to know him and that he was here?)	Jesus promised the New Testament.
expect him to leave earth in a different manner.	Jesus ascended bodily into heaven in full view of the disciples.

Add your own ideas. All asterisks in the chart above refer to material found in Josh McDowell's *Evidence That Demands a Verdict*.[5]

The point is that Jesus did exactly what you would expect God to do if he came to earth.

What We've Learned

When we add up the evidence, it's undeniable that Jesus directly claimed to be God. He did this not because he was crazy; he didn't do this to lie and deceive people; he did this for one and only one reason: He *is* God.

If someone says Jesus never claimed to be God, you can explain how he most certainly did.

One final question about the deity of Jesus remains. Is there any proof that he is God? Anyone can claim anything; proving it is something else. What's the evidence for his claim? That's the subject of our next chapter.

9

Is Jesus God? (Part II)

Challenge #7: "Jesus Didn't Prove He Is God"

Potential problem: Maybe Jesus did claim he was God, but if there's no proof, why should anyone believe it?

In January 2011, the Iranian government hanged a man named Abdolreza Gharabat. The execution made headlines around the world, and the crime was heresy: The man claimed to be God. He even had a small group of followers who believed he was God.[1]

The declaration itself *isn't* that unusual. Throughout history others have claimed the same. Egyptian pharaohs, Roman emperors, various kings, and plenty of self-proclaimed prophets all have said they were God. Some even demanded to be worshiped as such. The mere fact that Jesus said he was God isn't enough to prove it's true. Is there evidence that supports his assertion?

Proof That Jesus Is God

The evidence for Jesus' claim comes mostly from the New Testament. We have already seen that its documents are reliable, historical accounts written by men of high moral character (see chapter 7). Since this is true, we can trust what they recorded about the deity of Jesus Christ. What proof do they offer?

Proof #1: The New Testament Records the Virgin Birth of Jesus

In Luke's gospel we are told that the angel Gabriel appeared to Mary and told her she would have a son (see Luke 1:26–38). Mary was a virgin. She was engaged to Joseph, a righteous man. When Joseph found out Mary was pregnant, he determined not to take the matter public and wanted to quietly call off the wedding. However, an angel appeared to him and said that Mary was with child by a supernatural act of God (see Matthew 1:19–25).

What a stunning claim. Why would anyone invent something like this? Virgin births don't happen! But if it were true, it would be an act of God, and it could be offered as proof that Jesus truly is God.

Indeed, Jesus' claim to be God is *founded* on the fact of the virgin birth. It's recorded by Matthew, who knew Jesus personally. It's also recorded by Luke, who interviewed eyewitnesses before writing his gospel. Many scholars believe Mary was one of those to whom he spoke. Not only was Luke the author of a gospel account, he also was a doctor and a researcher of renown; he would have carefully examined a claim like this before reporting it as fact (see Luke 1:1–4).

By the manner of his birth, the New Testament affirms that Jesus is God.

Proof #2: The New Testament Records That Jesus Displayed the Attributes of God

An attribute is an *essential* part of someone's nature. By nature we are all part of humankind, so we all share certain attributes. One human attribute is that we all die. Another is that we all have limited knowledge—no human knows everything there is to know. We're also all limited in time and space—no human can be in two places at the same time. Even though we have different talents and different abilities, all people possess the same human attributes, because we are all equally human.

God, however, has a different set of attributes, which are described throughout the Old Testament. If Jesus is God, he should have the very attributes of God. As the following chart shows, he does.

Comparing the Attributes of God to the Attributes of Jesus

Attributes of God	Attributes of Jesus
God is eternal (Genesis 21:33).	Jesus is eternal (John 1:1–4).
God created everything (Genesis 1:1).	Jesus created everything (John 1:1–4).
God is life (Job 33:4).	Jesus is life (1 John 5:11).
God is an eternal ruler (Psalm 9:7).	Jesus is an eternal ruler (Hebrews 1:8).
God does not change (Malachi 3:6).	Jesus does not change (Hebrews 13:8).
God is present everywhere (Omnipresent) (Psalm 139:7).	Jesus is present everywhere (Omnipresent) (Matthew 18:20).
God knows everything (Omniscient) (Psalm 147:5).	Jesus knows everything (Omniscient) (Matthew 12:25).

Attributes of God	Attributes of Jesus
God is all-powerful (Omnipotent) (Jeremiah 32:27).	Jesus is all-powerful (Omnipotent) (John 13:3).
God has unique glory (Isaiah 42:8).	Jesus has God's glory (John 17:24).

If God possesses an attribute, Jesus possesses it as well. In terms of their nature, there is no difference between them. What God is, Jesus is; what Jesus is, God is; therefore, Jesus is God. Both the Old and New Testaments show this to be true.

Proof #3: The New Testament Records That Others Agreed Jesus Is God

GOD THE FATHER SAID JESUS IS HIS SON

At the baptism of Jesus, God the Father spoke from heaven and said, "This is my Son, whom I love" (Matthew 3:17). He said the same on another occasion (17:5). When the Father called Jesus "my Son," he was affirming the deity of Christ.

ANGELS PROCLAIMED JESUS AS GOD

Gabriel told Mary her child would be "the Son of the Most High . . . the Son of God" (Luke 1:32, 35). The angels who told the shepherds about his birth referred to him as "Lord" (2:11); lordship is an attribute of deity.

DEMONS RECOGNIZED JESUS CHRIST'S DEITY

Demons knew Jesus to be the "Son of God" (Matthew 8:29). They identified and acknowledged who he is, even if many of the people didn't.

THE DISCIPLES SAID JESUS IS THE SON OF GOD

Jesus' disciples knew him well. Here's how they described him:

Nathanael: "You are *the Son of God*; you are the king of Israel" (John 1:49).

Thomas: "*My Lord and my God!*" (John 20:28).

Peter: "You are the Messiah, *the Son of the living God*" (Matthew 16:16).

John: "Jesus is the Messiah, *the Son of God*" (John 20:31).

Jesus' Enemies Thought He Came From God

Even some of Christ's foes confessed that he was God. Nicodemus, a member of the Jewish high ruling council that would eventually vote to put Jesus to death, came one night to talk with him. During their conversation, Nicodemus admitted that the leaders, some of Jesus' strongest opponents, believed he was "a teacher who has come from God" (John 3:2). Though he probably was a polytheist, the Roman centurion who witnessed the crucifixion said, "Surely he was *the Son of God!*" (Matthew 27:54).

As recorded throughout the New Testament, a wide variety of people agreed and bore witness to the fact that Jesus is truly God.

Proof #4: The New Testament Records That Others Agreed Jesus Led a Sinless Life

If Jesus were God, he would have lived a perfect life (see chapter 8). God cannot sin, but what about Jesus? Many people attested to his perfect, sinless life.

It would be one thing if those who'd only heard about Jesus said he lived without sin. What about those who knew him best, though? What about those who walked, talked, ate, watched, listened, and lived with him? The two disciples most mentioned in the New Testament said the following about the man they knew so well: "He committed no sin, and no deceit was found in his mouth" (1 Peter 2:22); "He is righteous"; "He is pure" (1 John 2:29; 3:3).

While your friends may have a high view of you, your enemies usually don't. Consider the remarkable statements about Jesus by those who had no reason to make them unless they were true.

The Jewish leaders who rejected him said, "We know that you are a man of *integrity* and that you teach *the way of God* in accordance with the *truth*" (Matthew 22:16). Judas, who betrayed him, later confessed, "I have sinned . . . for I have betrayed *innocent* blood" (27:4). An officer who'd watched him die said, "Surely this was a *righteous* man" (Luke 23:47).

When Jesus was put on trial, even the highest Jewish officials were unable to produce any evidence against him. They had to manufacture false charges. They used false witnesses to convict him (Matthew 26:59–60).

When Jesus was brought before Pilate, he asked the Jews what crime he'd committed. They had no answer, and Pilate said, "I find no basis for a charge against this man" (Luke 23:4). Even Herod, who also examined Jesus after his arrest, said he'd "done nothing to deserve death" (v. 15).

The life of Jesus is a record of complete moral perfection. He loved all men. He loved *sinners*. He forgave his enemies while he was on the cross. Then this perfect man died without being convicted of any crime. He gave up his life to die for people like you and me. He said, "No one takes [my life] from me, but I lay it down of my own accord. I have authority to lay it down and authority to take it up again. This command I received from my Father" (John 10:18).

Jesus was "tempted in every way, just as we are—yet he did not sin" (Hebrews 4:15). No one who was merely a man could have lived such a life. The life of Jesus is proof that he is God.

Proof #5: The New Testament Records That Prophecy Proves Jesus to Be God

Another powerful proof that Jesus is God comes from prophecy. Biblical prophecy is not like popular psychic predictions, most of which never come to fulfillment. For example, the following people were predicted to die in 2010: Hugh Hefner, Queen Elizabeth, Ringo Starr, Billy Graham,[2] and Fidel Castro.[3] None of them did.

Some other predictions for 2010:

Angelina Jolie and Brad Pitt would split up. David Letterman would get divorced. Susan Boyle would get engaged.[4] The Empire State Building would come down.[5] There'd be another stock market crash.[6] A woman would claim to have had a son by Barack Obama.[7] There'd be an assassination attempt on the president, one that everyone would see.[8] None of these events happened.

The most common type of false prediction centers on the end of the world, the coming of the Antichrist, or the return of Jesus. Such "prophecies" have been made for centuries; obviously all have failed. Here's a tiny sample:

A variety of predictions have said Jesus would return, or the world would end, in the year 60, 90, 365, 400, 500, 968, 992, or 1000.[9]

Pope Innocent III predicted Christ would return in the year 1284.[10]

In 1669, Russian Christians believed the world's end was at hand. Twenty thousand burned themselves to death between 1669 and 1690 to protect themselves from the Antichrist.[11]

In 1835, Joseph Smith, founder of Mormonism, predicted Jesus would return before 1891.

In 1844, William Miller predicted Jesus would return that year. Many of his followers sold their possessions and quit their jobs.

In 1850, Ellen White, founder of Seventh-Day Adventism, said the world would end within a few months.

The Jehovah's Witnesses predicted the return of Jesus, or the battle of Armageddon, for 1914. When that failed, they predicted the same for 1915, then 1918, 1920, 1925, 1941, 1975, and 1994.

All these prophecies have failed, marking the men and women who made them as false prophets.

In contrast, biblical prophecy is 100 percent accurate. And the focus of many prophecies is Jesus Christ. At his first coming, Jesus fulfilled more than sixty, found in over three hundred references throughout the Old Testament.[12] These aren't vague or general predictions—they were detailed, and they were made centuries in advance. Some were very unusual and fit only one man. Let's look at a few to see the powerful prophetic evidence that Jesus is God.

Prophecies About Jesus' Ancestors

Beginning as far back as Genesis, there were predictions about ancestors of the Messiah. Initially broad, they became more and more specific as time went on. What started as a prophecy that he would come from the seed of a woman (Genesis 3:15), continued to include the line of Abraham (Genesis 12:1–3), then the tribe of Judah (Genesis 48:10), then the Son of David (2 Samuel 7), who would be born of a virgin (Isaiah 7:14) in the city of Bethlehem (Micah 5:1). Jesus fulfilled all of these prophecies perfectly.

Other Prophecies of His Birth, Life, Death, Resurrection, and Ascension

Here's a short list of other prophecies Jesus fulfilled in perfect detail.

Prophecies Fulfilled by Jesus

Prophecy	Fulfillment by Jesus
Messiah would be born in Bethlehem. Micah 5:2	Luke 2:4–7
Messiah would be born of a virgin. Isaiah 7:14	Matthew 1:23; Luke 2:5–11
Messiah would have a herald. Isaiah 40:3; Malachi 3:1	Matthew 3:3; Mark 1:2–3
Messiah would perform miracles and teach in parables. Isaiah 35:5–6; Psalm 78:2	John 10:32; 14:11; Matthew 13:10–13, 34–35
Messiah would enter Jerusalem on a donkey, on a certain day. Zechariah 9:9; Daniel 9:25	Matthew 21:1–5
Messiah would be forsaken by his disciples. Zechariah 13:7	Mark 14:50
Messiah would be silent before his accusers. Isaiah 53:7	Mark 15:3–5

Prophecy	Fulfillment by Jesus
Messiah would be wounded, sneered at, spit upon, and mocked. Isaiah 53:5–6; Psalm 22:7–8	Mark 15:19–20
Messiah would die around AD 33. Daniel 9:26	Luke 3:1 (AD 29, the fifteenth year of the reign of Tiberius, was when Jesus began his 3½-year ministry.)
Messiah would be crucified with rebels. Isaiah 53:12	Mark 15:27
Messiah would suffer and die for our sins. Isaiah 53:5–6	Matthew 26:28
Messiah's side would be pierced. Zechariah 12:10.	John 19:34–37
Messiah would have his garments parted and lots cast for them. Psalm 22:18	John 19:23–24
Messiah would be buried in a rich man's tomb. Isaiah 53:9	Mark 15:42–43
Messiah would rise from the dead. Psalm 16:10	Matthew 28:5–6; Acts 2:19–32

There are many more we could list, but even a skeptic should get the point. These detailed prophecies were made centuries before Jesus was born. Their fulfillment cannot be accidental or the result of chance.

JESUS SAID HE WAS THE FOCUS OF PROPHECY

Jesus clearly claimed he was the fulfillment of these ancient prophecies. He claimed the Old Testament prophecies were written about him. In fact, he said he came to fulfill them:

> Beginning with Moses and all the Prophets, he explained to them what was said in all the Scriptures *concerning himself*. (Luke 24:27)

> Everything must be *fulfilled* that is *written about me* in the Law of Moses, the Prophets and the Psalms. (Luke 24:44)

You study the Scriptures diligently because you think that in them you have eternal life. These are *the very Scriptures that testify about me.* (John 5:39)

Do not think that I have come to abolish the Law or the Prophets; I have not come to abolish them but *to fulfill them.* (Matthew 5:17)

Here I am—*it is written about me* in the scroll—I have come to do your will, my God. (Hebrews 10:7)

"THE MOST AMAZING PROPHECY"

Perhaps the most amazing prophecy is found in the book of Daniel. It is the "most amazing" because it proves that Jesus and only Jesus is Messiah. Many Jews still look for Messiah to come, but this prophecy shows he already has.

Here's the setting. The Jews had been conquered by Nebuchadnezzar's armies and taken away as captives to Babylon. Jerusalem and the temple were in ruins. Daniel knew from the writings of Jeremiah that the Jews would be in captivity seventy years, after which time God would bring them back to their homeland: "This is what the Lord [said]: 'When seventy years are completed for Babylon, I will come to you and fulfill my good promise to bring you back to this place'" (Jeremiah 29:10).

One day as Daniel prayed, he was interrupted by the angel Gabriel, who said he'd been sent to give Daniel special insight and understanding. The angel spoke of two time frames, far off in the future:

Know and understand this: *From* the time the word goes out to restore and rebuild Jerusalem *until* the Anointed One [Messiah], the ruler, comes, there will be seven "sevens," *and* sixty-two "sevens." . . . After the sixty-two "sevens," the Anointed One will be put to death and will have nothing. The people of the ruler who will come will destroy the city and the sanctuary. (Daniel 9:25–26)

The term *sevens* in the Bible can refer to seven days, seven months, or seven years. Here it refers to years. Gabriel identified two groups of seven years. One is a group of seven "sevens"; the other, a group of sixty-two "sevens." Let's do the math.

Multiplying 7 × 7 (seven groups of seven years each), we get a period of 49 years. Then, multiplying 7 × 62 (sixty-two groups of seven years each), we get a period of 434 years. Adding the two periods together gives a total of 483 years.

Daniel was told that these 483 years would begin at the issuing of the decree to restore and rebuild Jerusalem and would end with the coming of the "Anointed One, the ruler," that is, Messiah.

The beginning date for the fulfillment of this prophecy would be the issuing of a decree that allowed the Jews to go back and rebuild Jerusalem. We know the date on which that decree was given: King Artaxerxes issued it on March 5, 444 BC. That was the starting date, but when did the 483 years end?

By our present accounting of time—for several centuries we've been using the Gregorian calendar—the date would have come in AD 33.[13]

Why does it look like only 477 years would have elapsed (the last 444 "BC" years and the first "AD" 33 years) rather than 483? Because at the time, the accounting was made according to the Jewish calendar. The Jewish lunar year is 360 days, but our Gregorian calendar contains 365.25 days. Over the span of the days with the years of "sevens," there were about six more "Jewish years" than "Gregorian years." (The difference of 5.25 days per "year" means the Jewish calendar would have roughly 81 years for every 80 Gregorian years. Without listing more of the mathematical particulars here, the 483 [{7 × 7} + {7 × 62}] years of Daniel 9 equates to about 477 years of the calendar we use now.) So, this takes us to the very year Daniel predicted.

What happened on that date is what is important. Many scholars now agree that it was in the year AD 33 that Jesus (the "Anointed One" [Messiah], the ruler that Daniel had predicted) rode into Jerusalem on what we now call Palm Sunday. You can read about this event in Matthew 21:1–13; Mark 11:1–11; Luke 19:28–44; and John 12:12–19. Within just a few days of that event, the "Anointed One" was "put to death," as Daniel had also predicted. A prophecy made centuries in advance was fulfilled in detail by Jesus Christ.

DID JESUS SOMEHOW ARRANGE TO FAKE THE FULFILLMENT OF PROPHECY?

Some people say it only *seems* Jesus fulfilled a lot of ancient prophecies. The reality, they argue, is that he was a fake. Because he was a Jew, they contend, he would have known the prophecies about Messiah's coming. He only needed to be in the right spot at the right time, doing the right thing, and people would hail him as the "Anointed One."

But how could anyone do all this? How could you arrange to fulfill nearly sixty or more prophecies about Messiah's first coming? No one could arrange where they would be born. And certainly no one could arrange a virgin birth. How could you "arrange" to raise dead people or to heal the blind? And, most of all, *why* would anyone "arrange" to be betrayed, rejected, beaten, mocked, and then brutally, horrifically executed? If Jesus had "arranged" all these things, it certainly didn't end well for him. And he didn't get rich or live to enjoy any fame. This argument doesn't make sense.

THE IMPROBABILITY OF FULFILLED PROPHECY ABOUT JESUS

Is it possible Jesus could have arranged to fulfill what was foretold? Several studies have shown how impossible it would be for someone to fulfill even a few of these prophecies. Around the 1950s, over a span of several years, Dr. Peter Stoner gave his college students an assignment. He asked them to give the mathematical odds of one man fulfilling the following eight prophecies:

- Be born in Bethlehem

- Have a "forerunner" like John the Baptist

- Enter Jerusalem on a donkey

- Be betrayed by a friend

- Be betrayed for thirty pieces of silver

- Have the silver be used to buy "the potter's field"

- Refuse to defend himself

- Be crucified

About six hundred students participated in the project. When it was finished, Stoner took the estimates and rounded down the numbers. The odds of one man fulfilling just these eight prophecies: 1 in 10^{17}. That's 1 with eighteen zeroes after it. That's "one in 1,000,000,000,000,000,000."[14]

Stoner provided an illustration. Suppose you took enough silver dollars to cover the huge state of Texas up to two feet deep. Then mark just one coin, blindfold a man, and see if he can pick out the one you marked on his first try.

Good luck! Neither the odds nor the math is with you.[15]

Stoner also calculated the odds of one man fulfilling forty-eight out of sixty prophecies: one in 10^{157}. (Write this out for yourself if you want to take the time.) No one could have fulfilled these prophecies even if he wanted to.[16] He concluded: "Any man who rejects Christ as the Son of God is rejecting a fact proved perhaps more absolutely than any other fact in the world."[17]

Other studies have come up with similar odds, that is, yielded results akin to "no chance of happening." Professor Marvin Bittinger, bestseller of more than 12 million math texts, used the following example: Take a domed football stadium of average size and empty it of everything (stands, seats, lockers, et al.), then proceed to fill all remaining space with grains of white sand—white, except for one grain you've marked by coloring it red. What would be the odds of your selecting the same grain out of that whole stadium four times in succession? The answer is 1 in 10 to the 76th power.[18] This is a number so big that it's hard to fathom. Yet those are the odds of Jesus' fulfilling just *nine* prophecies about his coming. (Again, good luck!)

Fulfilled prophecy can be offered as powerful proof that Jesus is indeed who he claimed to be: the Son of God.

What We've Learned

We've looked at several fields of study, and we're building quite a list in support of the claims of Christianity. In this chapter we've seen a great deal of evidence that Jesus not only claimed to be God but also proved to be God.

Still, one question about Jesus remains: Did he truly rise from the dead? Many doubt the New Testament accounts that claim he came out of his tomb alive "on the third day." Therefore, we'll take one final look at the life of Jesus Christ and examine the evidence for his resurrection.

10

Jesus' Resurrection

Challenge #8: "Jesus Did Not Rise From the Dead"

Potential problem: If Jesus did not rise from the dead, he is a false prophet, and we cannot trust him, for he predicted his own resurrection. The New Testament writers claimed they saw the risen Jesus. If he did not rise from the dead, we cannot trust the New Testament either.

The Greatest Miracle Claim: A Man Rose From the Dead

The famous skeptic David Hume said, "It is no miracle that a man, seemingly in good health, should die on a sudden. . . . But it is a miracle that a dead man should come to life."[1] Of course, Hume didn't believe this ever happened, yet he raises a good point: Dead men don't come back to life.

There are accounts of people who claim to have returned after being declared clinically dead. Many books record their stories, and many of those books are popular. While such incidents have several different explanations, none is a true resurrection—at most they are resuscitations. We'll explain the differences shortly.

No matter what you may conclude about events like those, outside of the biblical claims for Jesus' resurrection, and his raising Lazarus from the dead (who later died again), no one has ever claimed that someone rose from the dead days after being declared dead and then buried.

The claim that Jesus rose from the grave is so spectacular that many explanations have been offered in an attempt to disprove it. Some say he passed out on the cross and later recovered. Once he recovered, say others, he ran off to France with Mary Magdalene, married her, had children by her, and eventually died a natural death. Others teach that Jesus went to (and died in) India. One town in Srinigar even claims Jesus is buried there. One member of a group known as the Jesus Seminar says Jesus died and later his body was dug up by dogs that ate it! Others speculate that the disciples moved his body. Still others suppose that thieves stole it. There are even a few who claim it vaporized in the tomb and vanished into thin air.

With all these notions about the resurrection, it's important that we know what really happened. *Did* Jesus die and rise again bodily? If he didn't, the Christian faith is based not on the greatest miracle but on the greatest fraud of all.

Jesus predicted his death and resurrection several times. For instance, he said, "The Son of Man is going to be delivered into the hands of men. They will kill him, and on the third day he will be raised to life" (Matthew 17:22–23; compare with 12:40; John 2:19–21). If he didn't come out of his tomb, he'd be a proven liar. He could not be God, and could not be our Savior. At best he'd turn out to be just like any other man, dead and gone. Christianity's central claim would be false and its founder a false prophet.

Here's what the apostle Paul said of what would be true in that case:

> If Christ has not been raised, *our preaching is useless* and *so is your faith.* More than that, we are then found to be *false witnesses* about God, for we have testified about God that he raised Christ from the dead. . . . And if Christ has not been raised, your faith is futile; *you are still in your sins.* (1 Corinthians 15:14–15, 17)

What Do We Mean by *Resurrection?*

People often confuse three terms: resuscitation, reincarnation, resurrection. Let's look at the differences.

When someone has experienced *resuscitation*—for example, had a heart attack but was later revived—he returns as the same man in the same body. He then will eventually die and be buried. After that, he will not come back.

Those who believe in *reincarnation* think that after you die, you come back as a different being in a different body. The theory also is that you come back again, and again, and again, and again, each time as a different being in a different body that eventually will die, and so on.

Resurrection means that someone who's died returns as the same person in the same body—only their resurrected body will be one that will never die again. The dying body has been changed into one that never again will face death.

Five Alternative Explanations for the Empty Tomb

Most Bible scholars, even critics who deny Christ's resurrection, agree that his tomb was found empty, days after his dead body was put there. Some, though, offer different explanations as to why it was empty. Here are some of the most common attempts to try and explain Jesus' empty tomb.

Explanation #1: Someone Else Died in Jesus' Place

Islam maintains that Jesus did not die on the cross. Muslims say Allah would not have allowed one of his prophets to die so awfully, so shamefully. Thus, Allah protected Jesus from death on the cross. Another explanation says this: Allah caused someone else to look like Jesus, and that person was crucified by mistake. Some Muslims believe it was Judas who was crucified.

Why Is This View Wrong?

There is no evidence to support this argument. It's based on one verse in the Qur'an (4:157) that showed up—with no eyewitness accounts—hundreds of years after the New Testament was written.

How could Jesus' mother and closest friends who were there not know the person on the cross wasn't him? No other man would go to the cross and not be screaming, *"You've got the wrong guy!"* Consider also the penalty for any Roman guard who made such a mistake.

Everyone involved with the death of Jesus had their own reasons to be absolutely certain it was really him on the cross. The Jews, the Romans, the soldiers, Pilate, even Jesus' own friends and family (who were *right there* at the cross) were all convinced it was Jesus who died there that day.

Those who knew him best watched him die. They had no doubt it was him. The men who buried him had no doubt. Anyone who believes otherwise is denying eyewitness testimony from a large group of people, all of whom agreed: It was truly Jesus who died on that cross.

Explanation #2: Jesus Only Fainted on the Cross; He Didn't Die

Proponents of this theory say that Jesus passed out on the cross and that everyone, even the trained soldiers, thought he was dead. After he was buried in the tomb, he revived, got out, and found the disciples, who mistakenly believed he'd been resurrected.

Why Is This View Wrong?

The response to this idea is simple: Jesus really died. We'll look at three different ways to prove it.

WHAT HAPPENED TO JESUS BEFORE HE WAS NAILED TO THE CROSS?

Before he was sent to die, Jesus was beaten. The rod the soldiers used was made up of several leather strips; each had pieces of embedded bone and/or metal that would tear into the flesh. They cut through capillaries, veins, and often arteries. They ripped apart muscles, could even slash intestines or other organs. A man's skin would become so damaged that the back of his body would become shredded. The spine might be exposed. There was an astounding loss of blood. Men passed out. Organs started to fail. Roman beatings were so brutal that many died from the beating alone.

155

By the time Jesus was sent to the cross, he'd been up all night. Probably he'd gone without food or water. And due to the beating, his body was so damaged that he couldn't carry the crossbar. He collapsed under its weight, and a man named Simon carried it. Mark tells us Jesus was "brought" to the cross—(this means "to carry"), so it's possible he was unable to walk. Jesus was severely weakened even before he was nailed to the cross.

What Happened to Jesus on the Cross?

For crucifixion, the Romans used specific procedures that were designed to insure that the condemned person would die. The whole point was to kill the offender. Here's a short account of what happened to a person on a Roman cross.

Hands and feet were nailed to the cross, which crushed nerves in hands and ankles.

Dehydration could become severe enough to cause death.

Bleeding from any prior beating continued while he hung there.

To survive awhile, he had to use his legs to push up his body so he could breathe; muscles began to cramp; nerves were further damaged.

Under the sagging body's weight, shoulders became dislocated.

Heart and lungs were under profound strain.

Jesus was on the cross more than six hours. No water, no food, no rest. His body was hideously debilitated.

The Romans kept trained eyes on men to note when they died. In the event a man didn't die soon enough, they would break his legs. Then he no longer could raise his body to breathe. Death followed quickly. When death was confirmed, death was pronounced.

In 1986, a group headed by William D. Edwards of the Mayo Clinic did a study on the death of Jesus. Edwards is a cardiovascular pathologist; he studies hearts, arteries, and veins in the human body. After examining the events surrounding the crucifixion, he concluded that Jesus was dead when he was taken down from the cross. He went on to say that anyone who believes Jesus did not die on the cross is "at odds with modern medical knowledge."[2]

In addition to modern evidence, we have this fact: Everyone who witnessed the event or was in any way involved agreed—Jesus died on that cross.

Witnessing his death were many of his friends, along with his mother and John, his closest follower. Women who knew him witnessed his burial. His disciples all believed he was dead.

Jewish leaders were there as well. They witnessed his death cry as he committed his spirit to God the Father.

The Roman soldiers, experienced with crucifixions, were so certain of Jesus' death that they didn't even follow the routine procedure of breaking his legs.

Pilate, surprised to hear that Jesus had already died, asked the Romans to check to be certain he was truly dead. Pilate refused to release Jesus' body for burial until he was certain of Jesus' death.

Nicodemus and Joseph of Arimathea, who buried Jesus, certainly were convinced he was dead. No one has ever suggested otherwise.

To grasp how absolutely sure people were that Jesus was dead, consider that in preparing a body for burial the Jews covered it with about a hundred pounds of spices, then wrapped it in linen strips and placed it inside a sealed tomb. If Jesus hadn't yet died, his burial would have ensured his death.

What Do Other Accounts Say About the Death of Jesus?

Other historical accounts also mention the death of Jesus. The Roman historian Thallus wrote about the darkness that fell upon the land during his crucifixion.[3] Another Roman historian, Phlegon, wrote: "Jesus . . . arose after death, and exhibited the marks of his punishment, and showed how his hands had been pierced by nails."[4] These men wrote matter-of-factly about Christ's death. They were not believers, and they had no reason to report something they did not believe was true.

These accounts agree: Jesus died on the cross. There's not one known account from that time that disputes his death—it's a solid fact based on eyewitness testimony of friend and foe, proven by the standards of modern medical evidence. Anyone who wants to pretend Jesus somehow survived the cross cannot point to *any* evidentiary data for support. He did not revive in the tomb, he did not run off to France, he did not make a life in India before dying there; Jesus Christ died in Jerusalem at Passover on a Roman cross.

Explanation #3: The Disciples Had a Mass Hallucination

Another argument against the resurrection says that the disciples had a mass hallucination, or a series of them, and only thought they saw the risen Jesus.

Why Is This View Wrong?

Hallucinations usually are caused by drugs, alcohol, lack of food, or lack of sleep. They normally last for a short time.

What if Jesus had survived?

Suppose for a minute this were true. Try answering these questions:

1. How did he manage to unwrap himself and get out of those graveclothes?
2. How did he move away the huge stone?
3. How did he manage to elude the Roman guards?
4. How did he find his disciples?
5. How could he convince his disciples he had risen from the dead? He would have been barely alive, and his body would have been a bloody mess.
6. How would a man who was in such a condition inspire the disciples?
7. Why did the disciples die—almost all suffering dreadful deaths—still claiming Jesus rose from the dead?

As one critic who denied the resurrection asked:

How could a man "who had [escaped] half-dead out of the [tomb], who . . . [was] weak and ill, wanting medical treatment, who required bandaging, strengthening and indulgence, and who still at last yielded to his sufferings . . . have given the disciples the impression that he was a Conqueror over death and the grave . . . ?"[5]

The same hallucination doesn't happen repeatedly. And as time passes, the hallucination fades and often is forgotten. They also happen to just one person. A hallucination is not like a cough—it's not contagious. The person having the hallucination can describe it to a friend, but the friend does not see it. Hallucinations are personal.

The disciples did not have a mass hallucination. They saw Jesus for long stretches, on at least twelve different occasions, over a forty-day period. They saw his crucifixion scars, touched him, talked with him, listened to him, ate with him for more than a month. Their conviction that he truly rose from the dead did not fade over time but stayed with them the rest of their lives. Almost all of them died as martyrs still proclaiming that they'd seen the risen Lord.

There is no evidence the appearances of Jesus were a mass hallucination.

Explanation #4: Somebody Moved or Stole the Body

Another popular theory is that someone took Jesus' body out of the tomb and moved it somewhere else.

Why Is This View Wrong?

Let's look at the number of obstacles anyone wanting to move Jesus' body would have had to overcome.

Pilate had ordered the tomb sealed and guarded. First, the "mover" would have to get past Roman soldiers. These were trained fighters, some of the world's best. They were heavily armed. During the night watch, one part of the group was always awake while others slept.

Roman guards did not leave their post. If they failed in their duty, they could be executed. Someone wanting to steal Jesus' body would have had to sneak by or fight a group of prepared, armed, trained fighters. Not likely.

Anyone trying to move Jesus' body also would confront the seal over the stone covering the tomb's entrance. The penalty for breaking a Roman seal could be death by crucifixion. Rome took grave-robbing very seriously.

Further, the "mover" would need a way to dislodge the massive stone in front of the tomb. In those days the stones used to seal a grave weighed between one and two *tons*. Matthew (27:60) and Mark (16:4) record that this stone was "big," "very large." The stone likely was wedged and rolled into the base of a trench at the opening. Removing it would have been a remarkable feat of strength and determination; accomplishing it would have made noise and taken time. How could they handle the guards and the stone simultaneously?

Who'd be crazy enough for the task? How many men would it have taken? Why would they risk their lives to do it?

The Jewish leaders? They were glad Jesus was dead and buried. They lacked a motive to move the body.

The disciples? They were terrified and in hiding. What could have compelled them to attempt it?

There's no evidence, and no explanation, as to why someone would have moved the body or how they could have done it.

When Jesus was buried, his body was wrapped in strips of linen cloth as myrrh and aloes were placed between the strips. A separate cloth covered his head.

The Egyptians used myrrh to embalm mummies. It hardened quickly and stuck to the strips, turning the linen into a kind of stiff cocoon. The rigid cloth and spices then stuck to the skin. How could anyone have removed this covering without destroying the skin and the linen? The body and the strips would have been a complete mess.

Yet when the disciples saw the empty tomb that Sunday morning, the linen was undisturbed, lying neatly in place. The head covering was separate, neatly folded up (Luke 24:12; John 20:5–7).

And when Jesus appeared to the disciples, his body was undamaged from having been embalmed.

Explanation #5: Jesus Organized a Resurrection Conspiracy Plot

One of the more far-fetched notions, known as "The Passover Plot," goes like this: Jesus, having become convinced that he was the Messiah, came up with an elaborate scheme to fulfill messianic prophecies, including a death by crucifixion. His plan was to be accepted by the Jews as their Messiah following a faked death and resurrection.

He found some Jews who agreed to help him. One arranged to give him drugs disguised as water while he was on the cross. The drugs made him unconscious; the Romans thought he was dead. The coconspirators would get his body after it was taken down and then nurse Jesus back to health.

After recovering, Jesus would claim to be resurrected. The plot failed, though, when he wound up dying from his wounds. The disciples who thought they saw him afterward had a case of mistaken identity. It wasn't Jesus.[6]

Why Is This View Wrong?

In chapter 9, we saw how impossible it would have been to try arranging to fulfill Old Testament prophecies. How could anyone arrange their city of birth or the tribe they were born into? How could you arrange miracles? Who would be willing to pretend they were blind, lame, or had leprosy and then be healed? Who'd believe them if they did?

There's absolutely no evidence for this explanation. It's entirely the result of someone's imaginative wishful thinking.

What We've Proved So Far

1. It really was Jesus on the cross.
2. Jesus really died on the cross.
3. Jesus' dead body was put in a sealed tomb.

Now we'll take a short look at some of the facts that support the historical, physical resurrection of Jesus Christ.

Some of the Facts That Establish Christ's Resurrection

The Tomb Was Found Empty

Even some very skeptical people admit that the evidence shows the tomb of Jesus was found to be empty within a few days of his death. Romans and Jews alike declared it was empty. Jesus' followers, both men and women, said the same. And if it hadn't been, why didn't the Jews and Romans enter the tomb and produce the body? The only answer is that it wasn't there. And it was never found anywhere else.

The only issue was how people explained the fact.

The Jewish leaders said the disciples came during the night and stole the body while the soldiers all slept (Matthew 28:11–15). The disciples said Jesus was resurrected. Whose explanation is correct? Here are some questions to help decide.

Why, just days after the crucifixion, would the disciples start boldly proclaiming a preposterous story they didn't believe? Again, these men had been in hiding, terrified, afraid for their lives—why would they suddenly put themselves on a life-or-death line preaching this in Jerusalem where it could have been easily disproven? How can you explain the fact that a large number of Jewish priests became Christians and believed Jesus rose from the dead within a short time after he was crucified? (See Acts 6:7.)

Best explanation: The disciples were telling the truth. Jesus truly had been raised.

There Were Multiple Eyewitnesses

Every one of the gospel writers, Matthew, Mark, Luke, and John, testify that men and women personally saw the risen body of Jesus. He bore the nail scars on his hands and feet and the mark where the Roman spear had pierced his side. Otherwise there was no evidence that he had even been crucified. He was not in a weakened condition. His body was not a bloody mess.

Jesus was with a variety of others on twelve separate occasions. He appeared to more than five hundred different people over forty days, indoors and outdoors, in Jerusalem and in Galilee. Some ate and drank with him. They talked with him. They touched his body. They saw his scars. They listened to him teach. They were with him until he ascended into heaven (see Acts 1:1–9).

Jesus even did miracles so there would be no doubt that it was him and that he'd been raised. Luke wrote, "After his suffering, he presented himself to them and gave many convincing proofs that he was alive" (Acts 1:3).

Virtually All of the Early Converts Were Jews in Jerusalem

Luke reported that within weeks of the crucifixion, thousands of Jews in Jerusalem converted to belief in Jesus; they believed he was the Son of God and that he'd been resurrected. Soon there were about five thousand Jewish Christian men (Acts 4:4), including many priests, in the city (6:7). Why did this happen so quickly? Why in Jerusalem, the heart of Judaism?

Think about what it would have meant for a Jew to become a follower of Jesus. He'd have had to become utterly convinced that Jesus was the promised Messiah, that he was God, and that he'd risen from the dead. After refusing for years to believe, why would all these Jews suddenly change their minds? Why would so many now take the word of the disciples that Jesus had been raised, unless they were certain it was true? Something most unusual and spectacular must have happened. Something like a man rising from the dead.

The Disciples Died for Their Belief in the Resurrection

Here's a short list of disciples who were martyred for preaching that Jesus was the Son of God and that he rose from the dead:

- Peter, Andrew, and Simon were all crucified.

- Matthew was killed by the sword.

- Mark was dragged to death by horses through Alexandria's streets.

- Luke died by hanging.

- James the Greater was beheaded.

- James the Just was thrown down from a pinnacle of the temple after refusing to deny Jesus Christ.

- Thaddaeus (sometimes known as Jude) was killed by arrows.

- Thomas was run through by a spear in India.

- Bartholomew (also known as Nathanael) was whipped to death in Armenia.

- Matthias was stoned and then beheaded.[7]

Read this account of Andrew's death. Does this sound like a man who had doubts about Jesus being raised from the dead?

Andrew was crucified in Greece after being whipped by seven soldiers. As he was being led to the cross, he said: "I have long desired and expected this happy hour. The cross has been consecrated by the body of Christ hanging on it." According to accounts that were left behind, Andrew did not die quickly; he lived for two more days, and preached from the cross to anyone who would listen until he finally died.[8]

Why would these men die agonizing deaths unless they knew for certain that what they believed was true? If they had any doubt Jesus was raised, surely one or more would have changed his story and saved his own life.

The Evidence Supports the Gospel Accounts

The evidence for the resurrection of Jesus Christ certainly has convinced many people who have taken the time to investigate it.

Sir Lionel Luckhoo was a famously successful defense attorney. The *Guinness Book of Records* (1990) cites him for having the most successive acquittals (245) in murder trials. This is what he said about the evidence for the resurrection of Jesus:

> I have spent more than 42 years as a defense trial lawyer appearing in many parts of the world and am still in active practice. I have been fortunate to secure a number of successes in jury trials and I say unequivocally the evidence for the Resurrection of Jesus Christ is so overwhelming that it compels acceptance by proof which leaves *absolutely no room for doubt*[9] (emphasis added).

And many who'd initially refused to accept the resurrection have become convinced of its historicity and accepted Jesus as Lord and Savior.

What We've Learned

In this chapter we've seen that:

1. Jesus was crucified and died on a Roman cross.
2. His body was embalmed in linen and spices.
3. He was buried in a tomb that was sealed and guarded.
4. Days later that tomb was found empty.
5. The disciples saw the living Jesus many different times.
6. Their lives were completely, permanently changed by their conviction that he rose from the dead.
7. They preached this in Jerusalem right away.
8. Many Jews became believers.
9. Not one of the disciples ever recanted his belief that Jesus was raised.
10. Most of them died as martyrs for their faith.

In light of the evidence, here's the question we should ask skeptics: "What happened in Jerusalem two thousand years ago that so changed the disciples that they were willing to die for their belief in the resurrection?" The only answer can be that they actually saw the risen Lord. They did not have a mass hallucination. They weren't part of some grand plot. They saw the living Jesus Christ following his death on the cross.

Considering the Three Theistic Religions

Judaism, Christianity, and Islam all maintain that God exists and that he created everything. They agree that God is the Beginner, the Designer, the Moral Lawmaker. Now it's time to ask how each matches the facts we've considered about the New Testament documents and Jesus Christ.

Based on the evidence for the reliability of the New Testament, for the claims of Jesus to be God, for the proof that Jesus is God, and for the evidence for the resurrection, we must rule out Judaism and Islam.

Neither Judaism nor Islam affirms Jesus as God. Remember the law of noncontradiction that says two contradictory truth claims cannot both be true at the same time? The evidence shows that Jesus both claimed and proved to be God. Therefore, it cannot be true that he is not God. Also, the evidence shows that he was raised from the dead, so it cannot be true that he was not raised from the dead. Someone here is right, and the others are wrong. Based on the evidence alone, we must conclude that Judaism and Islam are incorrect in what they maintain about the New Testament and the nature, life, death, and resurrection of Jesus.

Comparing the Three Theistic Religions

Issue	Christianity	Judaism	Islam
New Testament documents	The New Testament documents are reliable.	Jews do not accept the New Testament accounts.	Islam believes the New Testament documents are corrupt. They are not reliable.
Did Jesus claim to be God?	Yes.	Jews may agree that Jesus claimed this, but they do not agree that he is God.	Jesus did not claim to be God, he was merely a man who was a great prophet of Allah.
Did Jesus prove to be God?	Yes.	No.	No.
Did Jesus rise from the dead?	Yes.	No.	No. Many Muslims believe Jesus did not die at all. Someone took his place on the cross. Allah took him to heaven, and Jesus will return one day and die at some point in the future.

By denying Christ's deity, death, and resurrection, many sincere Jews and Muslims have turned their backs on God's gracious provision of salvation through Jesus' sacrifice. We are to pray for all who do not know that Jesus truly is God. We need to share with them the evidence that he is. We must make known the Good News: Not only did he die for the sins of the whole world, but he also proved he is God by rising from the dead.

Some people still insist that other religions also have the truth. They do not believe that God has revealed himself to us only through the Bible. How should we answer them? That's what we'll consider next.

Other Religious Books

Challenge #9: "The Bible Isn't the Only True Religious Book"

Potential problem: Is there truth in other religious books? If so, what does that mean for Christians?

This is a valid question, one we must answer. Christians believe the Bible is true, but is it possible that other religious books are true as well? If there's truth in other religious books, would that pose a problem for followers of Jesus Christ?

Consider these points:

1. God, the Moral Lawmaker, cannot lie; he keeps his own moral law.
2. Jesus both claimed and proved to be God.
3. Whatever Jesus teaches must be true, since he is God (who cannot lie).

4. Jesus taught that the Bible is God's Word.
5. Therefore, the Bible is God's Word.

This means anything in any other religious book cannot be true *if it contradicts the Bible*, for contradictory truth claims can't both be true. Because Jesus is God, and because he taught that the Bible is the Word of God, if something contradicts the Bible, it is wrong. Let's examine what Jesus said.

What Did Jesus Teach About the Old Testament?

Jesus referred to the Old Testament with words like *Scripture, Word of God,* and *Law and Prophets*, and with the phrase "It is written." To the Jews, these terms were clear references to what we call the Old Testament.

What *did* Jesus have to say about the Old Testament? Is it God's Word?

Jesus Quoted the Old Testament as Having Divine Authority

Many times Jesus quoted from the Old Testament, sometimes prefacing it with "It is written" (e.g., Matthew 4:4, 7, 10). Each time, he was validating the Old Testament's authority. He used it to rebuke the devil, to exhort the Jewish leaders, and to establish his own authority as being sent from God. Jesus confirmed the Old Testament's authority as *God's* Word.

Jesus Said the Scriptures Are Unbreakable

Jesus said "Scripture" (the Old Testament) could not be broken or set aside (John 10:35). He taught that God's Word cannot change or fail in any manner—it's actually unbreakable. As the psalmist said, "Your word, LORD, is eternal; it stands firm in the heavens" (Psalm 119:89).

Jesus Said the Bible Is Imperishable

Jesus believed the Scriptures are literally indestructible:

Do not think that I have come to abolish the Law or the Prophets; I have not come to abolish them but to fulfill them. For truly I tell you, until heaven and earth disappear, not the smallest letter, not the least stroke of a pen, will by any means disappear from the Law until everything is accomplished. (Matthew 5:17–18)

Jesus Said the Old Testament Is True

On one occasion, Jesus rebuked some of the Jewish religious leaders. They were discussing what happens after we're resurrected and, in particular, debating the question "Is there marriage in heaven?" Jesus said they were wrong if they believed in marriage after death: "*You* are in error because you do not know the Scriptures or the power of God" (Matthew 22:29). The Old Testament was not wrong; they were wrong. The Old Testament is true.

The night he was betrayed, Jesus told his disciples that God's Word (the Old Testament) "is truth" (John 17:17). The psalmist said, "All your words are true" (Psalm 119:160).

Jesus Said the Old Testament Accounts Are Historically Reliable

Today's critics deny the Bible's account of creation. They don't believe God created humankind. They also deny the flood at the time of Noah, and they reject the claim that Jonah was swallowed by a large fish.

Jesus, however, treated all these accounts as historically true.

Speaking to a group of Pharisees one day, he said, "At the beginning of creation God 'made them male and female'" (Mark 10:6). He was affirming that humankind is a separate creative act of God. We didn't evolve by "natural forces," and Adam and Eve were real, historical people, the first of their kind.

Jesus confirmed there was indeed a flood in Noah's time: "As it was in the days of Noah, so it will be at the coming of the Son of Man. For in the days before the flood, people were eating and drinking, marrying and giving in marriage, up to the day Noah entered the ark" (Matthew 24:37–38).

Jesus was also clear about Jonah: "As Jonah was three days and three nights in the belly of a huge fish, so the Son of Man will be three days and three nights in the heart of the earth" (Matthew 12:40).

Today these are some of the most disputed, most discounted parts of the Old Testament. Jesus treated them as fact, as historical truth.

Jesus Taught That the Bible Is Scientifically Accurate

It's common today to hear people insist that we're the result of millions of years of gradual evolution and deny any possibility that we were created. Jesus, however, said that both men and women were created:

Haven't you read . . . that at the beginning the Creator "made them male and female," and said, "For this reason a man will

174

leave his father and mother and be united to his wife, and the two will become one flesh" (Matthew 19:4–5)?

Jesus Said the Bible Is Ultimately Supreme

Because the Jewish leaders had put their interpretations above God's Word itself, Jesus rebuked them: "Why do you break the command of God for the sake of your tradition?" (Matthew 15:3); "Thus you nullify the word of God by your tradition that you have handed down" (Mark 7:13).

Jesus showed that the Bible is the final, supreme word on everything it teaches, *the* authority on what we should believe and how we should behave.

Jesus Said He Came to Fulfill the Old Testament Prophecies

Jesus said that the Old Testament spoke of him: "You study the Scriptures diligently because you think that in them you have eternal life. These are the very Scriptures that testify about me, yet you refuse to come to me to have life" (John 5:39–40). "Beginning with Moses and all the Prophets, he explained to them what was said in all the Scriptures concerning himself" (Luke 24:27).

In his Sermon on the Mount he said he came to fulfill the Old Testament prophecies (Matthew 5:17). On several occasions he explained that his upcoming death and resurrection would be a fulfillment of Scripture:

> Jesus took the Twelve aside and told them, "We are going up to Jerusalem, and everything that is written by the prophets about the Son of Man will be fulfilled. He will be delivered over to the Gentiles. They will mock him, insult him and spit

on him; they will flog him and kill him. On the third day he will rise again" (Luke 18:31–33).

He treated the prophetic sections of the Old Testament as guarantees that would be fulfilled.

According to Jesus, the Old Testament is from God. It can be trusted. It won't fail or break. It's historically accurate, and many of its prophecies were fulfilled at his first coming. Since Jesus is God, we can trust what he says.

Jesus didn't hesitate to point out the faults of leaders, calling them hypocrites and blind guides who hurt the poor. Yet he never charged them with corrupting their Scriptures; instead he affirmed the Scriptures' reliability.

Is There Other Evidence Confirming the Old Testament?

How about additional evidence that proves the Old Testament to be reliable? Here are four lines of support for its trustworthiness.

Ancient Manuscripts Demonstrate That the Old Testament Has Been Copied Accurately

We've looked at manuscript support for the New Testament. Several pieces of evidence show the Old Testament is equally well preserved.[1]

First, the Jewish scribes who copied their Scriptures were *very* careful. They counted every word and every letter in every line. They even located the middle letter in the center of each line and compared it to the manuscript they were reproducing to see if everything lined up. Scribes could not write or copy from memory. They had to check and work from a previously approved manuscript. If an error was found, the page would be destroyed.

Second, in 1947, ancient copies of the Old Testament were discovered. Known as the Dead Sea Scrolls, these are evidence that the Old Testament manuscripts have been accurately preserved.

Take, for example, the book of Isaiah, one of the Old Testament's longer books. A copy with all sixty-six of its chapters was found among these scrolls, which was one thousand years older than any prior surviving copy of Isaiah.

Once scholars had the chance to compare it to what had previously been the oldest copy, they found the book of Isaiah had been preserved through all those centuries word-for-word, with 95 percent accuracy. Most of the rest were spelling and grammatical errors, but none affected the teaching of any passage.

Third, the English bishop Benjamin Kennicott, a Hebrew expert, did an extensive study to determine Old Testament accuracy. He studied 581 manuscripts, involving some 280,000,000 letters. His conclusion: The Old Testament had been reliably copied more than 99 percent of the time. Most "mistakes" dealt with pronunciation and spelling. Not one affected the text's basic message.[2]

Archaeology Supports the Old Testament's Reliability

Archaeology has proved the Old Testament's historical reliability. Here are some of the things archaeologists have uncovered:

- The tomb of Abraham in Machpelah has been found in modern-day Hebron. Jews, Christians, and Muslims visit it today.

- The city of Jericho with its fallen walls has been uncovered in the exact spot the Bible describes.

- The destroyed cities of Sodom and Gomorrah, along with their charred homes, have been uncovered in layers of thick ash.

- Evidence of ancient peoples, including the Hittites (mentioned many times in the Old Testament), has been found. Even their capital city has been excavated.

- The tunnel Hezekiah built has been found. Tourists walk through it from one end to the other. (See 2 Kings 20:20.)

- Evidence for the temple in Jerusalem has been uncovered.

- Evidence for King David has been found.

Many discoveries have proven that the Old Testament is a reliable historical document. No archaeological find has ever disproved any Old Testament truth claim. A *U.S. News & World Report* feature said, "In extraordinary ways, modern archaeology has affirmed the historical core of the Old and New Testaments—corroborating key portions of the stories of Israel's patriarchs, the Exodus, the Davidic monarchy, and the life and times of Jesus."[3]

Fulfilled Prophecies Show That the Old Testament Is True

We've already seen that Jesus fulfilled more than sixty individual prophecies found in the Old Testament. These were detailed predictions that were perfectly fulfilled. Other prophecies were completely fulfilled as well.

For instance, following the fall of Jerusalem, around 650 BC, the nation of Israel was taken captive and marched all the way to Babylon. It was a horrible time for the Jews and a cause for great despair. Yet Jeremiah prophesied that their captivity would last only seventy years:

> This is what the LORD says: "*When seventy years are completed* for Babylon, I will come to you and fulfill my good promise to bring you back to this place" (Jeremiah 29:10).

Isaiah added to this prophecy, saying that a man named Cyrus would eventually appear on the scene. When he showed up, he would allow the Jews to return to their former homeland and rebuild their temple:

> *Cyrus* . . . will say of Jerusalem, "Let it be rebuilt,"
> and of the temple, "Let its foundations be laid" (Isaiah 44:28).

These prophecies, like the others, were fulfilled. Ezra recorded that when the seventy years were over,

> In the first year of *Cyrus* king of Persia, *in order to fulfill the word of the LORD* spoken by Jeremiah, the LORD moved the heart of Cyrus king of Persia to make a proclamation throughout his realm and to also put it in writing:

> This is what Cyrus king of Persia says: "The LORD, the God of heaven, has given me all the kingdoms of the earth and *he has appointed me to build a temple for him at Jerusalem in Judah*" (Ezra 1:1–2).

More recently, we've seen prophecy fulfilled when Israel became an independent state in 1948. God promised his people almost three thousand years ago that one day he would bring them back to their land:

> Even if you have been banished to the most distant land under the heavens, from there *the LORD your God will gather you and bring you back. He will bring you to the land that belonged to your ancestors, and you will take possession of it.* (Deuteronomy 30:4–5)

Men Would Have Written the Old Testament Differently

The "heroes" of the Old Testament were by no means always admirable. Noah got drunk. Abraham didn't trust God to fulfill his promise that a son would be born to him by his wife, so to "help God out," he had a son by his wife's servant. Moses murdered a man. David committed adultery with Bathsheba and then had her husband murdered.

The Jews were freed from Egypt and witnessed great miracles from God. But they quickly turned to idols and would do so again and again throughout their history. Their kings and leaders worshiped pagan gods and even offered their little children to them, burning them alive to show their devotion. Prophets, like Jonah, ran away.

This is not a pretty picture. Yet it's an accurate portrait of real people. Why would anyone record a history of such moral and spiritual failure unless it was true? If we were making all this up, we'd invent more heroic heroes.

There are many reasons the Old Testament can be trusted as a reliable, accurate, historical record that has been faithfully preserved.

Was Jesus Just Accommodating Jewish Beliefs?

When faced with all this evidence, some critics respond by claiming that Jesus' view of Scripture was simply his way of adapting to, adjusting to, or fitting in with commonly accepted (but false) Jewish beliefs of his day.

This is known as the "accommodation theory." Let's see how it fares.

Was Jesus an accommodator? *Did* he try to adapt to the popular beliefs of his times, to modify his views to harmonize with religious or political leaders?

All the evidence says no. Consider the facts for yourself, and ask yourself if you think they show Jesus to be an accommodator of false teachings.

Jesus Rebuked Those Who Set Their Traditions Above God's Word

Jesus asked the Pharisees and scribes, "Why do you break the command of God for the sake of your tradition? . . . You nullify the word of God for the sake of your tradition" (Matthew 15:3, 6).

Jesus Placed His Word Against False Views on God's Word

Jesus corrected incorrect teachings. He repeatedly said to the Jews, "You have heard that it was said . . . but I tell you" (Matthew 5:21–22, 27–28, 31–34, 38–39, 43–44), thus rebuking the false teachings they had based on the Old Testament.

Jesus Rebuked Nicodemus, a Highly Placed Jewish Rabbi

Jesus said, "You are Israel's teacher . . . and do you not understand these things? . . . I have spoken to you of earthly things and you do not believe; how then will you believe if I speak of heavenly things?" (John 3:10, 12).

Jesus Declared That the Powerful Sadducees Were Mistaken

The false beliefs of the Sadducees included the denial of any future resurrection. Jesus told them flatly, "You are in error because you do not know the Scriptures or the power of God" (Matthew 22:29).

Jesus Boldly and Publicly Denounced Religious Leaders

Woe to you, teachers of the law and Pharisees, you hypocrites! You travel over land and sea to win a single convert, and when you have succeeded, you make them twice as much a child of hell as you are.

. . . You say, "If anyone swears by the temple, it means nothing; but anyone who swears by the gold of the temple is bound by that oath." You blind fools! Which is greater: the gold, or the temple that makes the gold sacred? . . .

. . . You give a tenth of your spices—mint, dill and cumin. But you have neglected the more important matters of the law—justice, mercy and faithfulness. . . . You strain out a gnat but swallow a camel.

. . . You clean the outside of the cup and dish, but inside they are full of greed and self-indulgence. Blind Pharisee! First clean the inside of the cup and dish, and then the outside also will be clean.

. . . You build tombs for the prophets and decorate the graves of the righteous. And you say, "If we had lived in the days of our ancestors, we would not have taken part with them in shedding the blood of the prophets." So you testify against yourselves that you are the descendants of those who murdered the prophets. Go ahead, then, and complete what your ancestors started!

You snakes! You brood of vipers! How will you escape being condemned to hell? (Matthew 23:15–17, 23–26, 29–33)

Jesus Took Strong and Decisive Action in Cleansing the Temple

He made a whip out of cords, and drove all from the temple courts, both sheep and cattle; he scattered the coins of the money changers and overturned their tables. To those who sold doves he said, "Get these out of here! Stop turning my Father's house into a market!" (John 2:15–16).

Even Jesus' Enemies Recognized That He Did Not Compromise or Bend His Views to "Get Along With" or Accommodate Anyone

The Pharisees and the Herodians, who both opposed Jesus, said to him:

Teacher . . . we know that you are a man of integrity and that you teach the way of God in accordance with the truth. You aren't swayed by others, because you pay no attention to who they are. (Matthew 22:16)

What Did Jesus Teach About the New Testament?

The New Testament hadn't been written in Jesus' day. But the night he was betrayed, he spoke to his disciples about what would happen when he was gone, promising that his Spirit would come and help them in four specific ways. The result of these four promises would be the New Testament.

Jesus Said the Holy Spirit Would Teach Them "All Things"

"The Advocate, the Holy Spirit, whom the Father will send in my name, will teach you all things" (John 14:26). Jesus promised that his Spirit would be their teacher and would teach them everything they needed to know. Nothing would be withheld. The Holy Spirit is the Spirit of God. God, in the person of the Holy Spirit, would personally teach the disciples.

Jesus Said the Holy Spirit Would Guide Them Into "All Truth"

Jesus said that not only would his Spirit teach them, but also, "When he, the Spirit of truth, comes, he will guide you into all the truth" (John 16:12–13). Nothing would be overlooked. What eventually became the New Testament would include everything the disciples needed to know and record. The Spirit of God would direct them and reveal it to them.

Jesus Said the Holy Spirit Would Remind Them of Everything He Had Said to Them

Jesus promised the disciples they would be reminded by his Spirit of everything they'd heard and seen while he was with them—it would all be brought back to their memory. The Spirit "will remind you of everything I have said to you" (John 14:26).

Jesus Said the Holy Spirit Would Tell Them What Is Yet to Come

Finally, Jesus told the disciples his Spirit would reveal future events to them, "will tell you what is yet to come" (John 16:13). Some of those present that evening, like Peter and

John, would record prophetic events that God will one day fulfill. They did so under the Spirit's inspiration and guidance.

That night, the last night Jesus was alone with his disciples before he was crucified, he laid the foundation for the New Testament. He told them they would be the ones to record his words and the events of his life. They would be given the ability to accurately recall what they had seen and heard by the Spirit's power. The Holy Spirit is God; the New Testament would be written and compiled under the guidance of God himself.

The New Testament Is the Only Contemporary Record of What Jesus Taught

Almost all scholars now agree that the entire New Testament was written in the first century, when the apostles and eyewitnesses were still alive. In fact, it is the only record coming from the time of the apostles that contains what they taught. Since Jesus promised he would lead them into "all the truth" and "bring to their remembrance" what he taught, it follows that their writings are the fulfillment of his promise. The Bible is finished, complete. We need no additional revelation from God. We have the whole story.

Conclusion: Jesus Confirmed the Reliability of the Old Testament and Promised the New Testament

Remember, because Jesus is God, the following statements are true:

1. Whatever Jesus (God) teaches is true.
2. Jesus taught that the Bible is the Word of God.
3. Therefore, the Bible *is* the Word of God.

Can't Other Religious Books *Also* Contain Truth?

This is an important question since many people today believe there's truth in all religions. To answer it, we have to go back to one of the first points we made.

In chapter 2, we looked at one of reality's unbreakable laws, the law of noncontradiction, which states: Contradictory truth claims cannot both be true at the same time and in the same sense. We have seen that the Bible is true. So then, to the extent that any other book contradicts it, it is false.

Let's look at four key areas. We'll examine what other religions teach about God, about Jesus, about his resurrection, and about how we are saved.

What Do Other Religions Teach About God?

The Bible says that only one knowable, personal God exists—a theistic God. Pantheism says "god," or a god-force, flows through everything. Polytheism, by definition, upholds many different gods (e.g., Hinduism). Buddhism also denies the existence of one personal, knowable God. Since a theistic God exists (see chapters 3–5), and since the Bible is true (see above), pantheism, polytheism, and Buddhism are wrong about the nature of God.

What Do Other Religions Teach About Jesus?

The Bible teaches that Jesus is uniquely and eternally God. Jews, Hindus, Buddhists, and Muslims deny this. Pantheists and polytheists believe he was a man who became God (or a man who came to realize he is God), and that all people can become or realize that they are God. Accordingly, to them, Jesus is not unique, and he has not always been God.

Mormonism also teaches that Jesus was a man who became God, and that devout Mormons can become gods after they die. Jehovah's Witnesses believe Jesus was Michael the archangel, a created being. These beliefs all contradict the Bible. If the Bible is true, and it is, these teachings are false.

What Do Other Religions Teach About Jesus' Resurrection?

Pantheism, polytheism, and atheism deny any resurrection. Judaism, Buddhism, and Islam deny Jesus rose from the dead.

Jehovah's Witnesses teach that Jesus did not rise bodily from the dead. Rather, they allege, only his spirit was raised; the disciples only saw a "re-created" body. They did not see a risen Jesus in the same physical body in which he died.

By denying the physical, bodily resurrection of Christ, these religions and their documents contradict the Bible, which has been shown to be true.

What Do Other Religions Teach About How We Are Saved?

Christianity teaches that all people are sinners and that the penalty for sin is death. All the good works in the world cannot change this. None of us, not even the best of us, can undo the consequences of sin.

But God has done something about this. When Jesus died on the cross, he paid our penalty for sin; he died in our place, shedding his blood and giving his life as a sacrifice for us. He could do this because he is God, and our sins can be forgiven because of what he accomplished. We are saved from the penalty of sin when we accept Jesus as our Savior, acknowledging that we are sinners and that we need the salvation only he can provide.

"The wages of sin is death, but the gift of God is eternal life in Christ Jesus our Lord" (Romans 6:23). No human being could ever deserve or earn something like this. The price was Christ's death on the cross. All we have to do is accept God's present to us—it's free, just open the package!

Other religions teach that good works are necessary to attain salvation. Hindus work hard to be good in order to be reincarnated into a better life next time around. Buddhists try to be moral people in hopes of being absorbed into Nirvana. Muslims say prayers five times daily, fast, tithe, and go on pilgrimages in hopes of gaining paradise. Mormons hope they've been good enough to reach heaven's highest level. Jehovah's Witnesses believe just 144,000 of them will make it to heaven.

Only Christianity teaches that we cannot earn our salvation (Ephesians 2:8–9). Any faith that teaches that you must earn the right to go to heaven, or paradise, or the highest of heavens, contradicts the Bible. Therefore, other religions are wrong about how and why people will get to heaven.

It's not hard to see that the texts of other religions contradict the key claims of the Christian faith. The Vedas and Upanishads (Hinduism), the Pali Canon (Buddhism), the Qur'an (Islam), the *Book of Mormon* and *Doctrine and Covenants* (Mormonism), and the Watchtower's literature (Jehovah's Witnesses) all contradict the Bible, and wherever they do, they are incorrect.

See the chart at the end of this chapter for a summary of the ways in which other religious texts contradict the Bible.

Not Everything Other Religions Teach Is Wrong

Other religions have teachings and beliefs that *don't* contradict the Bible. In fact, for the most part, as we saw in chapter 4, religions share a common moral code. This is because God has given all people a moral conscience (Romans 2:12–15). Moral truth found *anywhere* is evidence of a Moral Lawmaker.

Creation also bears witness to the fact that there is a God who created the universe. He has left his fingerprints for all to see. Paul tells us that God's eternal power and divine nature are clearly seen in the world around us (Romans 1:19–20). We learn that he is divine. He is not us, and we are not him. Various aspects of these truths are found in various belief systems.

The bottom line is this: The opposite of true is false. The Bible is true, therefore, any claim from any source that contradicts it (is the opposite of what it teaches) is false. And since truth itself flows from God's own nature, so all truth is his, no matter where we find it.

What We've Learned

We've looked at three ways to respond to the question of whether truth can be found in other religions.

First, Jesus is God, and God cannot lie, so whatever Jesus teaches is true. Jesus taught that the Bible is God's Word, thus the Bible is the Word of God.

Second, we reviewed the law of noncontradiction and noted that because the Bible is the Word of God, nothing that contradicts it can be true.

Third, there can be truth in other faiths, for God has left evidence of who he is in our conscience and in creation.

We've looked long and hard at the *evidence* that shows Christianity is true. It's not popular today to say other religious books are wrong, but it's true that they are. Contradictory truth claims *can't* both be true, no matter who wants them to be.

This is a sobering thought. There are people we know and love who are lost, and without God cannot spend eternity in heaven with him. Many are not willing to accept this. Many continue to believe that, somehow, all good people with sincere beliefs will be welcomed into heaven.

This is the final objection we'll examine. Can good, sincere people get to heaven without accepting Jesus as their Savior? *Is* Jesus the only way to God?

Some of Christianity's Unique Truth Claims

Take a look at this chart to see how unique the claims of Christianity are. These truth claims separate Christianity from all other religions:

Christian Truth Claims	Other Religions' Claims
1. All men are sinners.	1. Men are just weak, or bad. If they try hard enough, they can be good.
2. Sin separates us from God, and we cannot do anything to find or reach God on our own. Men cannot get to heaven by doing good deeds.	2. If we are sincere, do good deeds, and try hard to be better, we will find God and go to heaven.
3. God is the only one who could fix the problem of sin. He did it by sending Jesus to die for our sins.	3. God does not fix us; he does not save us. We must save ourselves by trying hard to be good.
4. Jesus died for us; he took our place; he was our substitute and paid the penalty for sin (death).	4. No one can take our place. We must pay for our own bad deeds, for our own weak nature, by becoming better people.
5. We must put our faith in Jesus to be saved and go to heaven.	5. We put our faith in some kind of god and our good works.
6. Jesus is the only source of eternal life.	6. Jesus does not give us eternal life. We must earn it.
7. Jesus is the only way to God.	7. There are many paths to God. Just be sincere, try hard, and be good.

Because the Bible Is True, Whatever Contradicts It Is False

Bible	Atheism	Deism	Pantheism Hinduism	Buddhism	Judaism	Islam	Mormons	Jehovah's Witnesses
Only one knowable, personal God exists.	Disagrees. There is no God.	Partial agreement. There is one God, but he is not involved in the world.	Disagrees. There is one non-personal God (Brahman) and many gods.	Disagrees.	Agrees.	Partial agreement. Allah is not personal, knowable.	Disagrees. Mormons can become gods.	Agrees.
Miracles are possible.	Disagrees. There is no God to perform a miracle.	Disagrees. No miracles take place.	Disagrees. All is natural. There is no supernatural.	Disagrees. There is no supernatural realm.	Agrees.	Agrees.	Agrees.	Agrees.
Only Jesus is eternally, uniquely God.	Disagrees. Jesus is not God.	Possible. But deny the virgin birth, resurrection.	Disagrees. There are many gods.	Disagrees.	Disagrees. Jesus is not God.	Disagrees. Jesus is merely a great prophet.	Disagrees. Jesus is a man who became a god.	Disagrees. Jesus was originally an angel.
Jesus rose from the dead.	Disagrees.	Disagrees. Miracles are not possible.	Disagrees. Jesus was reincarnated.	Disagrees.	Disagrees.	Disagrees.	Agrees.	Disagrees. Jesus was not raised bodily.
Only the Old and New Testaments are from God.	Disagrees. Neither is from God, from man only.	Possible. But, they deny all miracle accounts.	Disagrees. Their holy books are the Vedas, Upanishads.	Disagrees. Their book is known as the Pali Canon.	Disagrees. Only the Old Testament qualifies.	Disagrees. The Bible is corrupt. The Qur'an replaces it.	Disagrees. The Bible is corrupted. Need Book of Mormon, Doctrine and Covenants, and others.	Agrees, but have a different Bible translation, and have prophetic voice.

An "agree" answer means they agree with the Bible on this point. If what we have proved is correct, every "disagree" answer violates the law of non-contradiction. Therefore, each of these belief systems is false. Look for the "disagree" answers to see how many places each belief system contradicts Christianity and the Bible.

$$\textbf{12}$$

Is Jesus the Only Way to God?

Challenge #10: "Christianity Is Too Narrow.
There Are Many Ways to God Besides Jesus"

Potential problem: If there are other ways to God besides Jesus, then the Bible is wrong, and Jesus did not speak the truth.

We've spent several chapters examining Jesus and the Bible. We've learned that Jesus, as God, validated the entire Bible as being God's Word. With this in mind, consider the following statements he made about how people can find God and spend eternity in heaven with him:

I am the way and the truth and the life. No one comes to the Father except through me. (John 14:6)

Very truly I tell you . . . anyone who does not enter the sheep pen by the gate, but climbs in by some other way, is a thief and a robber. . . . I am *the gate*; whoever enters through me will be saved. They will come in and go out, and find pasture. (John 10:1, 9)

This is a clear claim. If you want to find God, Jesus says he alone is the way.

Peter, John, and Paul agreed:

Salvation is found in no one else, for there is no other name under heaven given to mankind by which we must be saved. (Acts 4:12)

Whoever has the Son has life; whoever does not have the Son of God does not have life. (1 John 5:12)

There is one God and one mediator between God and mankind, the man Christ Jesus. (1 Timothy 2:5)

If Jesus says he is the one way to God, and if the New Testament writers agree, then on the basis of our established conclusions, we can know that Jesus is the one way people will find the one true God and have a relationship with him.

Some Popular Ideas About Reality and Salvation

Many today do not believe Jesus is the only way to God. Many chafe at the thought that this could be true, and many say that those who do believe it are narrow-minded, arrogant, and/or intolerant. Many find it offensive that Christians claim to know the truth. Many suppose that all religions have part of the truth and that all sincere people will go to heaven. Many admit that Jesus is *a* way to God, but surely he cannot be *the* way.

On this crucial issue, Oprah Winfrey has said:

I believe that there are many paths to God. Or, many paths
to the light. I certainly don't believe that there is only one
way. There couldn't possibly be just one way [to God]. . . .
There couldn't possibly be with the millions of people in the
world. . . . Does God care about your heart, or does God care
about if you call his Son Jesus?[1]

You might be inclined to dismiss Oprah's views on the
grounds that she's only a prominent media personality. But
even some prominent ministers don't believe Jesus is the only
way to God. Katharine Jefferts Schori, the twenty-sixth presiding bishop of the Episcopal Church in the United States,
expressed her stance on the matter in a 2005 interview:

Christians understand that Jesus is the route to God. That is
not to say that Muslims, or Sikhs, or Jains come to God in
a radically different way. They come to God through human
experience—through human experience of the divine. We
who practice the Christian tradition understand him as our
vehicle to the divine. . . . But for us to assume that God could
not act in other ways is, I think, to put God in an awfully
small box.[2]

Oprah, once more:

One of the mistakes that human beings make is believing
that there is only one way to live. . . . There are millions of
ways to be a human being, and many ways, now, many paths
to what you call God. And her [Betty Eadie, her guest] path
might be something else. And when she gets there, she might
call it the light. But her loving, and her kindness, and her
generosity—if it brings her to the same point that it brings

you, it doesn't matter whether she called it God along the way or not.[3]

This widespread belief goes something like the following: Everyone who endeavors to be good and sincerely believes that their own ideas about God are true will go to heaven. God is big on sincerity, so whatever you understand or think about God, if you truly have faith and are committed to your beliefs, everything will turn out fine for you at the end of life.

This is why it's common to hear people say things like:

- "All roads can bring us to heaven."

- "We're all going up the same mountain—we're just taking different paths to the top."

- "Everyone's on their own journey, but all good people will arrive at the same destination."

Such statements encourage us to think it doesn't matter what we believe. Any "good" person will find it all works out in the end. God just needs to know you've been *good*. If you've tried hard to be good, he's happy and will reward your efforts.

Another important factor is being *sincere*. It's not necessary to believe anything in particular about God or to hold a particular faith. You need to be "a good person who sincerely believes whatever you believe."

One example that's used to illustrate the value many people today place on sincerity is found in a story known as "The Blind Men and the Elephant." Six blind men are asked to touch an elephant and explain what they think it is.

One man touches the tusk and says it's a spear. The second finds the trunk and thinks it's a snake. The third feels the leg and says it must be a tree. The fourth grabs the tail and says he's holding a rope. Man number five finds the elephant's ear and concludes it's a fan. The last man pats the elephant's side and says he's found a wall.

Professors and teachers often use this story to demonstrate how sincere people may reach different conclusions about the same object. In the case of the six blind men, no matter that they reached different conclusions—they were all touching the same elephant! Therefore, they're *all* "right," it's just a matter of perspective, point of view, or understanding.

The professor or teacher may go on to say that we're just like these men. Even when we have different ideas about God, we're all touching him. Whatever God you choose to worship, or whatever you believe about God, it's all the same God in the end.

However, this illustration has a major flaw. The elephant is not a spear, a snake, a tree, a rope, a fan, *or* a wall. *None* of the men came to the correct conclusion; *all* were wrong. The reason they were wrong is that they were blind. If they could see, they would not only know the truth—that they were touching an elephant—but they would also know they had come to a wrong conclusion.

The same thing is true of our beliefs: If my premises are wrong, my conclusion will be wrong too. If my beliefs about Jesus are wrong, I'll reach the wrong conclusion about who he is. If I reach the wrong conclusion about who Jesus is, it won't matter how "sincere" I am, how "good" I am, or how "hard" I've tried. I will have erred tragically and inevitably, regardless.

Sincerity, in itself, isn't the point. If I'm sincerely *wrong*, my sincerity is misdirected. I can sincerely believe the world is flat. But neither my belief nor my sincerity will make a bit of difference. The world is what it is—round—and no amount of zeal or fervency will change that reality.

In the case of the six blind men, coming to the wrong conclusion wasn't a fatal mistake. It didn't affect their destiny. But if the Bible is true, if Jesus is God, and if he is the only way to God, then being wrong and remaining sincerely wrong about the Bible and Jesus and eternity will affect everything.

Let's do a quick review of what we've learned about Jesus and the reliability of his words.

What We've Demonstrated About Jesus

Jesus *did* claim to be God. He accepted worship and honor due to God alone. And he proved to be God through his virgin birth, sinless life, miracles, and resurrection. We've also seen that prophecy proves Jesus to be God.

What We've Shown About the Bible

Jesus, who is God and therefore cannot lie, taught that the Bible is God's Word. He confirmed the reliability of the Old Testament and promised the New. Many New Testament writers were eyewitnesses of the events they recorded. The men who recorded those events told the truth. The Old and New Testament documents have been accurately preserved and are reliable historical records.

Facts That Support Jesus' Claim to Be the Only Way to God

Only Jesus Died on the Cross for Our Sins

Muhammad did not die for anyone. Neither did Buddha, Krishna, or Joseph Smith. By contrast, Jesus died for all people. The penalty for sin is death and eternal separation from God. But the Bible is clear: Jesus, the sinless Son of God, died in our place and paid the penalty for our sins:

John [the Baptist] saw Jesus coming toward him and said, "Look, the Lamb of God, who *takes away the sin* of the world!" (John 1:29).

I [Jesus] am the good shepherd. The good shepherd *lays down his life for the sheep*. (John 10:11)

God demonstrates his own love for us in this: While we were still sinners, *Christ died for us*. (Romans 5:8)

Christ *died for our sins* according to the Scriptures. (1 Corinthians 15:3)

He is the atoning sacrifice for our sins, and not only for ours but also *for the sins of the whole world*. (1 John 2:2)

"He himself *bore our sins*" in his body on the cross, so that we might die to sins and live for righteousness; "by his wounds you have been healed" (1 Peter 2:24).

No one but Jesus took our place and paid the price for us. Only Christianity maintains that Jesus died for the sins of all. Every other religion contradicts this truth claim.

Only Jesus Saves

Only the Bible says we cannot earn our salvation. We cannot save ourselves; only Jesus can rescue us from the penalty of sin. All other religions contradict this truth claim, mandating good deeds and/or setting other conditions.

> [We] are *justified freely by his grace* through the redemption that came by Christ Jesus. (Romans 3:24)

> It is by grace you have been saved, through faith—and this is not from yourselves, *it is the gift of God—not by works,* so that no one can boast. (Ephesians 2:8–9)

> *[Jesus] saved us, not because of righteous things we had done, but because of his mercy.* He saved us through the washing of rebirth and renewal by the Holy Spirit. (Titus 3:5)

Only Jesus Promises Us Eternal Life as a Free Gift

No one else can give us eternal life; it only comes from Jesus.

> God so loved the world that he gave his one and only Son, that whoever believes in him shall not perish but have *eternal life*. (John 3:16)

> My Father's will is that everyone who looks to the Son and believes in him shall have *eternal life*, and I will raise them up at the last day. (John 6:40)

> The wages of sin is death, but the gift of God is *eternal life* in Christ Jesus our Lord. (Romans 6:23)

No other person except Jesus has ever personally offered people eternal life. All other religions contradict this truth claim.

Only Jesus Asks Us to Put All Our Faith in Him

Jesus wants us to place our faith and our hope entirely in him. Muslims highly revere Muhammad, but they do not believe Muhammad can save them.

> Whoever *believes in the Son* has eternal life, but whoever rejects the Son will not see life, for God's wrath remains on them. (John 3:36)

> If you do not *believe that I am he* [the one I claim to be], you will indeed die in your sins. (John 8:24)

All other religions contradict this claim. Therefore, we must now rule out two of the three theistic religions: Islam and Judaism. They both contradict the core beliefs of Christianity. Christianity is the only theistic religion left standing.

Chart 12.1
Ruling out Islam and Judaism

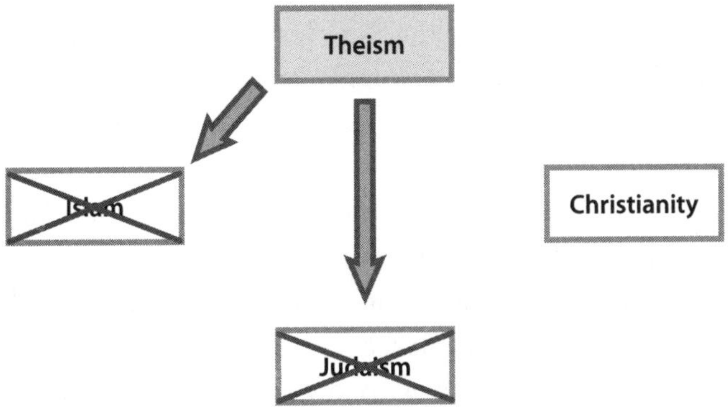

(For a short comparison of religious leaders, see the chart at the end of this chapter. Jesus stands in *contradiction* to all others.)

Isn't It Narrow-Minded to Say Jesus Is the Only Way to God?

All other religions contradict every core New Testament claim about Jesus. For the final time, we're brought back to the reminder that contradictory truth claims *cannot* both be true. Look one more time at these statements to see how clear they are about Jesus being the only way to God:

> I am the way and the truth and the life. No one comes to the Father except through me. (John 14:6)

> Salvation is found in no one else, for there is no other name under heaven given to mankind by which we must be saved. (Acts 4:12)

> Whoever has the Son has life; whoever does not have the Son of God does not have life. (1 John 5:12)

These declarations are unambiguous. They're either true or false. Either Jesus and the New Testament writers are right or they are wrong. We must make our choice.

If Jesus is God, he cannot be wrong. If Jesus is not God, then he is wrong on the most important matter—how we can have our sins forgiven—and we cannot trust what he says. If he is not God, he would not be the way, the truth, and the life, and he would not be the only way to the Father. In fact, if he did not speak the truth, he is not even *a* way to the Father—he is not a way to anywhere.

But again, as we've seen, Jesus *is* God. His words *are* true.

Here the laws of logic compel us all to make a choice: a choice about Jesus. If his claims to be God are true, and thus his claim to be the only way to God is true, then everything that contradicts him is false. The claim that he is the only way to God is no more narrow-minded, closed-minded, arrogant, or intolerant than any other belief someone may hold, for *whatever* they believe to be true, the opposite of it must be false.

And so the only real question is *"Is it true that Jesus is the only way to God?"* For all the reasons we've stated above, this claim is demonstrably true. Now you must ask yourself, "What am I going to do about it?" You have a decision to make.

True or false? Right or wrong? *What do you say of Jesus and his claims?*

C. S. Lewis, who understood the laws of logic, challenged us to make a decision about the claims of Jesus. Are they true or false?

> You must make your choice. Either this man was, and is, the Son of God, or else a madman or something worse. You can shut Him up for a fool, you can spit at Him and kill Him as a demon, or you can fall at His feet and call Him Lord and God. But let us not come with any patronizing nonsense about His being a great human teacher. He has not left that open to us. He did not intend to.[4]

Lewis is right. The law of noncontradiction insists that we choose. Jesus is the only way to God, or he is not. There is no other option.

What About People Who Have Never Heard of Jesus?

Here is one question you may be asked when talking with someone about Jesus: "How can people who have never heard of him come to God if Jesus is the only way?" Sometimes the one who asks is truly concerned and wants to know what would happen to someone who really wanted to follow the one true God but has never heard about Jesus. Here are a few facts that may help you respond to this objection.

Perhaps the most important point to stress is that God *wants* all people to come to him. To help us find him, he has revealed something of his nature and character in what he has made. What can we learn of him from creation?

Since the creation of the world God's invisible qualities—his *eternal power* and *divine nature*—have been clearly seen, being understood from what has been made, so that people are without excuse. (Romans 1:20)

The heavens proclaim his *righteousness,* for he is a God of *justice.* (Psalm 50:6)

The heavens praise your *wonders,* LORD, your *faithfulness* too. (Psalm 89:5)

Lift up your eyes and look to the heavens: Who created all these? He who brings out the starry host one by one and calls forth each of them by name. Because of his *great power and mighty strength,* not one of them is missing. (Isaiah 40:26)

Ah, Sovereign LORD, you have made the heavens and the earth by your great power and outstretched arm. *Nothing is too hard for you.* (Jeremiah 32:17)

In the beginning, Lord, you laid the foundations of the earth, and the heavens are the *work of your hands.* (Hebrews 1:10)

The heavens declare the glory of God; *the skies proclaim the work of his hands.* Day after day they pour forth speech; night after night they reveal knowledge. They have no speech, they use no words; no sound is heard from them. Yet *their voice goes out into all the earth, their words to the ends of the world.* (Psalm 19:1–4)

God has left a witness that can speak to all people, at all times, in all places. Creation informs us that a powerful, supremely intelligent, faithful, all-powerful, righteous, Divine Being *exists* and that he made everything we see. God has left a witness in the work of his hands that has pointed many men and women to him who had no prior knowledge of the true God, yet they deduced that he must be there and wanted to know him.

Still, people worry that some who want to know God won't be able to find him. The truth is we need *not* worry about this. Any person living at any time or in any place who is seeking for the true God will find him.

I love those who love me, and those who seek me *find me.* (Proverbs 8:17)

From one man he made all the nations, that they should inhabit the whole earth; and he marked out their appointed times in history and the boundaries of their lands. *God did this so that they would seek him and perhaps reach out for him and find him,* though he is not far from any one of us. (Acts 17:26–27)

Without faith it is impossible to please God, because *anyone who comes to him must believe that he exists and that he rewards those who earnestly seek him.* (Hebrews 11:6)

People who seek him will find him because of these truths: First, God knows all things; he knows the hearts of all people, and he knows anyone who is seeking him.

[God] *knows* the secrets of the heart. (Psalm 44:21)

The LORD looks down from heaven on all mankind to see if there are any who understand, any who seek God. (Psalm 14:2)

Nothing in all creation is hidden from God's sight. (Hebrews 4:13)

Second, God is all-powerful, able to reach all people.

I am the LORD, the God of all mankind. *Is anything too hard for me?* (Jeremiah 32:27)

Jesus looked at them and said, "With man this is impossible, but *with God all things are possible*" (Matthew 19:26).

Third, God is all-loving; he wants all people to be saved. He pleaded with his people to turn from their waywardness and come to him.

As surely as I live, declares the Sovereign LORD, I take no pleasure in the death of the wicked, but rather that they turn from their ways and live. Turn! Turn from your evil ways! Why will you die, people of Israel? (Ezekiel 33:11)

Jesus invites *everyone, everywhere*, to come to him:

Whoever comes to me I will never drive away. (John 6:37)

Come to me, *all* you who are weary and burdened, and I will give you rest. (Matthew 11:28)

Peter also reminds us of God's desire that all people would be saved:

The Lord is not slow in keeping his promise, as some understand slowness. Instead he is patient with you, *not wanting anyone to perish,* but everyone to come to repentance. (2 Peter 3:9)

One day, standing before God's throne in heaven, there will be people from every tribe, language group, ethnic group, and nation (see Revelation 7:9). Think about this. Throughout history there have been *many* tribes, language groups, ethnic groups, and nations. What an astonishing thought—not *one* people group that has ever been on the face of the earth will be excluded. Once again: Everyone, from any locale, in any era, who seeks God can find him. God loves us; God wants to bring us to himself. If someone wants to know God, God will see that the gospel of Jesus Christ is brought to them.

Salvation is offered to everyone. There's no IQ test—people of any mental capacity can accept Jesus. There's no age restriction—little children can accept Jesus, as can people at the end of their life. There's no financial requirement—it doesn't matter what we have or don't have. We needn't be recognized for having remarkable abilities or talents. And it doesn't matter where we are—the one true God will find any man, woman, or child who desires a relationship with him. That person will come to know him through Jesus Christ.

The all-powerful God is not limited by conventional means. Missionaries have documented many unusual and even dramatic ways that true seekers, in some very dark places, spiritually speaking, have received the message of Jesus. God desires to use missionaries, but he can and has spoken to people through a Bible passage, a gospel tract, an angel, a vision, or a dream. Many accounts have been preserved in Don Richardson's *Eternity in Their Hearts* (Regal, 2006). Read it and you'll see just a few of the ways God has reached those who've chosen to seek him. Also see Emir Fethi Caner and H. Edward Pruitt's *The Costly Call* (books 1 and 2, Kregel, 2005 and 2006).

Does someone want to know God? God knows it, and he will get his Word to them. Jesus invites *all* to come to him. There *is* only one way through one Savior to the one true God. And that way is open to *everyone*.

The choice is yours. We all make a choice—for or against—the Bible, the God of the Bible, and Jesus Christ. Centuries ago a man named Joshua made his choice to follow the one true God:

> If serving the LORD seems undesirable to you, then *choose* for yourselves this day whom you will serve. . . . But as for me and my household, we will serve the LORD. (Joshua 24:15)

Having completed our examination of the evidence for Christianity, there are two final questions we'll address in our last chapter:

How can I give a better answer for why I follow Jesus?
How should the truth impact my daily life?

Comparing Great Religious Leaders—How Unique Jesus Is!

Characteristic	Jesus	Muhammad	Buddha	Confucius	Joseph Smith
Virgin born?	Yes.	No such claim was ever made. His father and his mother both were known to his tribe.	No such claim was ever made.	No such claim was ever made.	No such claim was ever made.
Sinless?	Yes.	No. He asked to be forgiven in the Qur'an: 48:1–2.	No such claim was ever made.	No such claim was ever made.	No such claim was ever made.
Made prophecies?	Yes. And, they were all fulfilled.	Some predictions, not detailed, good guesses. Some failed.	No.	No.	Yes, but they failed to come true.
Did miracles?	Yes. Many different types, many eyewitnesses. Also raised the dead.	Refused to do miracles. Claims show up very late. Some are weird, mimic miracles of Jesus. No eyewitness accounts.	No.	No.	No.
Resurrected?	Yes.	No such claim was ever made. His tomb is a known site with a body in it.	No such claim was ever made.	No such claim was ever made.	No such claim was ever made.
Ethical standard?	The highest: The Golden Rule, the Sermon on the Mount. Love your enemies, do good to those who hate you. Turn the other cheek, give away your coat.	Some ethics. You must follow Muhammad's ethics. But he broke every one of the Ten Commandments. Problems with treatment of women. Does not come even close to the level of Jesus' ethical standards.	Silver Rule: "Don't do to others as you don't want them to do to you." Good, but not as strong as Jesus' ethical standards.	Good, moral advice, but not as strong as Jesus' ethical standards.	Practiced polygamy, even against his wife's wishes. Involved with the occult. Misrepresented his knowledge of reformed Egyptian.

13

How Should the Truth Impact My Life?

What Does the Evidence Mean for Me?

In light of all the evidence that shows Christianity to be true, we need to ask two final questions. First, how can we give a better answer to the question "Why are you a Christian?" Second, how should the truth impact our daily life? How should all the truths we've examined change each one of us?

How Can I Give a Better Answer for Why I Follow Jesus?

The Bible admonishes Christians to be prepared to give an answer to anyone who wants to know why we believe:

> Always be prepared to give an answer to everyone who asks you to give the reason for the hope that you have. But do this with gentleness and respect. (1 Peter 3:15)

So how ready are you to answer this important question? If you feel you're not adequately prepared to explain the support for your faith, here are a few practical suggestions that may be of help.

First, ask yourself where you need to grow intellectually in your understanding of Christianity's core beliefs. Make a list of areas where you have questions. Do you need help talking to a friend who belongs to another faith? Do you need a better handle on what makes your beliefs unique? Do you struggle with questions about evil? Write down each topic you think you need to learn more about. Then state each area as a question. For example, if you wanted to know more about the evidence for God, you might write it out like this: "How can I *know* God exists?" Or "What *is* the evidence that the God of the Bible is really there?"

Second, prioritize your list of questions. What's the most important area right now for you to study and learn more about? Sometimes our list is long, and we can't tackle all the areas at once. Arrange them in the order of their importance to you.

Third, seek out some resources that will help you gain understanding in each area you listed. At the end of the chapter, we'll list some helpful sources. You can also talk to your pastor, Bible study leader, or other trusted believers for help in locating good books, DVDs, CDs, articles, and more. (Many are available at *www.normangeisler.net*.)

Fourth, take the questions you've written and begin to record an answer to each. (This will take time. It doesn't happen quickly. Your answers are likely to expand and develop as you learn.) Then read your answers aloud, as if you were talking to someone. If you have a friend or family member you can practice on, read your answers aloud to them. This will help you organize your thoughts and answers for the time when you may be asked these questions. Growing in your faith and learning to give better, more complete answers is a lifelong process, but you *will* make progress—as long as you choose to start and then keep going. Don't allow yourself to believe that this is too difficult. You actually will learn a great deal within a short period of time.

As your knowledge, wisdom, and adeptness increase, remember that your ultimate purpose is not to try to impress anyone with how much you know. It is not to win arguments or simply to become a skilled debater (though God can use well-prepared debaters). Your purpose is to point people to the one true God through his Son, Jesus Christ. Humbly present your mind to God and ask him to use it. Don't try to defeat others; rather, seek to win them to God through Jesus.

This prompts a question. How many nonbelieving friends do you have? None? One? Just a few? The Christian life is not meant to be lived inside a Christian fortress solely with your Christian friends. We all need to get up, get out, and reach out to a dying world that desperately needs Jesus.

If you have no such friends in your life right now, prayerfully ask God to bring some into your life. Then make an effort to reach out and make new friends. Do you go to school—to whom might you extend friendship there? Do you have a job—what colleague(s) could you befriend? If you don't know where to start, what about your neighbors—can you invite them into your home and get to know them? Can you join a hobby group or special-interest group? If you go to the gym, whom do you meet? Be creative, and then be willing to be a true friend to anyone God places in your path.

God may choose someone you might not have chosen, or he may put someone there who, from your perspective, is a bit rough around the edges. God often has his own ideas about whom we are to befriend. *Everyone* needs a Christian friend who can model the love of Jesus Christ and impact their life.

God has called all followers of Jesus to be lights in a dark world. Jesus said so (Matthew 5:14); we're to be a "guide for the blind, a light for those who are in the dark" (Romans 2:19). We all need to be available to minister the love and grace of Jesus to anyone who may come our way.

How Should the Truth Impact My Daily Life?

One day a teacher of the Jewish law came to Jesus and asked him to sum up all the laws into one simple command. In addition to the Ten Commandments, in an endeavor to apply the law in their daily life, the Jews added an additional 613 mandates to govern everything they did.[1] It had become a never-ending heavy burden to try to keep up with—and to keep—all the details. So this man asked, "Of all the commandments, which is the most important?" (Mark 12:28). Jesus replied:

> Love the Lord your God with all your heart and with all your soul and with all your mind and with all your strength. (Mark 12:30)

Easy, right? Shouldn't loving God be a simple thing to do? Well, Jesus chose a very special term to describe *how* we are to love God. In the Greek language, several words describe different levels of love and commitment. The one used here, *agape* [ah-GAH-pay], describes love's highest form. *Agape* means to love someone totally and completely. It means to love them not because of what they can do for us or because of what we might hope to get from them, but just for who and what they are.

Jesus wants us to love God so completely that we are willing to commit our whole lives to him, that we become devoted to his will and purpose. This kind of love is not merely on a check-off list ("I loved God today"). It's a choice we make moment by moment, day by day, to place our entire being—thoughts, desires, plans, choices—at his feet for his service.

Jesus not only tells us to love God, but he also tells us *how* to love him. We are to love God with all our heart, mind, strength, and soul.

What does this mean? What would it look like to love God in this way?

I Am to Love God With All My Heart

In saying that we are to love God with all our heart, Jesus is obviously not referring to the physical organ that beats in our chest. He's pointing to the center of human desires and emotions. Our heart, as Jesus used it, is where we make choices, where we decide how to think and what to do. It's the part of us that chooses to do right or wrong, good or evil. It's where we decide whether or not to please God, whether or not to follow and obey him.[2]

Loving God with all our heart means we make decisions that please him. If I truly love someone, I will choose to do what would please them. I will choose to honor them. So if

215

I say I love God, I will make choices that honor him. I will obey him and seek his will for my life.

This is an area on which Christians normally put much emphasis. Pastors talk a lot about loving God and making choices that please him. But we can't overlook the other three ways in which Jesus commands us to love God.

I Am to Love God With All My Mind

What does Jesus mean to love God with all our mind? We rarely, if ever, hear anyone talk about this aspect of his command, yet clearly we're to use our mind in a particular way if we claim we love God.

Further, no one is exempt—this is a command for all believers, not just those with a certain IQ. It's not just for those who are older, or for those who may have more time to study. God has given each of us a mind and wants us to use it as part of loving him better and more completely.

Our mind is where we think, where we reason, where we come to conclusions.[3] Paul *reasoned* from the Scriptures (see Acts 17:2–3), debating with facts as he encouraged people to reach a conclusion about the risen Jesus.

Christian faith is not blind faith; it always has content. God expects us to take in information, think about it, analyze it, and then arrive at a conclusion about whether or not it is true. He has given each of us a mind, and he expects us to use it in loving him.

Here are some points we've covered that involve the use of our mind:

1. We must *understand* the nature of truth and how we can know it.

216

2. We must *understand* that there are correct and incorrect ways to think. God has created each of us as a rational being with the capacity to think correctly. The laws of logic help us in this area.
3. We must *understand* and remember and be able to explain the evidence for God.
4. We must *understand* why miracles are possible.
5. We must *understand* why both the Old and New Testaments are accurate, reliable, trustworthy documents.
6. We must *understand* that Jesus claimed and proved to be God, that he was raised from the dead, and that he is the only way to God.

Loving God with all your mind means you have considered the evidence for Christ's deity and have accepted who he is. It means you've examined the evidence for the truth of God's Word and accepted its claims. It means you've weighed the evidence for God's existence and accepted that he truly exists.

Having examined much evidence showing Christianity to be true, what are your conclusions? If you believe this evidence, if you've accepted it as true, you're on the way to loving God with all your mind. As you grow in your understanding of his Word, of the truth, your ability to love him with all your mind will increase and grow as the days go by.

I Am to Love God With All My Strength

When Jesus tells us to love God with all our strength, he's not referring to physical strength. Instead, he's asking us if we have the spiritual strength to take a stand for him. Do we have the strength, spiritually speaking, to live by his moral standard?

Do we have the intellectual strength to defend the truth of his Word and not back down when someone attacks it?[4]

Our world presents countless moral challenges. Standards and guidelines are overlooked or broken. Cheating and lying are sufficiently commonplace to be seen as an acceptable way to deal with parents, spouses, or friends. Many choose to have sex outside of marriage. Language deteriorates and coarsens; in many quarters, taking God's name in vain provokes no reaction. Young people defy parents; older people ignore and fail to take care of aging parents. People crave what others have and often see no wrong in taking it.

Christians also face many intellectual challenges, for which they may be unprepared. Atheists, agnostics, humanists, members of other religions, as well as cults present truth claims that make many believers question their faith. Many who are not sure how to respond simply retreat.

No wonder some decide to spend time only with other Christians. Maybe they find it too difficult to challenge popular culture. Perhaps they don't know how to answer the challenges. Many think there are just "too many issues" and conclude that no one is strong enough to stand for God today.

But think about this. When Noah was the only righteous man left on earth, he still stood for God. Abraham's and Lot's families were living among a pagan culture that rejected the true God, yet they stood for him. Two men, Moses and Aaron, took on the political and religious system of the whole Egyptian empire. Three men—Shadrach, Meshach, and Abednego—faced excruciating death but still refused to bow to a mighty king. The apostles were beaten, flogged, and hunted; most were gruesomely martyred because they chose to stand for Jesus. God used each of these individuals in their time and place because of just one thing: They found the strength to stand for him.

God calls all of us to become strong enough to stand for him. He's called us to be salt and light to a world that, spiritually, is rotting and dark (Matthew 5:13–16; Romans 2:19). Are we willing to love him with all our strength by taking an uncompromising stand for him, even when we're afraid, even when we don't feel like it? Are you willing to stand for God even when you think he doesn't know best? Are you willing to bend your will to his—to submit to his guidance and to his clear directives? Are you willing to obey him even if you struggle with what he commands? Even when you don't yet understand it?

God calls us to live a unique lifestyle, a *holy* lifestyle. God often says, "Be holy, because I am holy."[5] We normally think *holy* means to be morally pure, to be perfect, and that certainly is one meaning. However, *holiness* also means to be set apart—separate from something.[6] For example, as God's people live *within* a given culture, we're to be different from it—to be separate from it—morally. We're to live our lives according to his standard.

Will you build the courage to choose a righteous lifestyle over a popular one? Do you have the courage to make righteous choices in an unrighteous culture? Noah and Lot did. They were both called righteous men even though they lived in a culture that was anything but righteous.

Noah was a righteous man, *blameless* among the people of his time. (Genesis 6:9)

[Lot was] a *righteous* man, who was distressed by the depraved conduct of the lawless. (2 Peter 2:7–8)

Do you have the courage to make a difficult choice? Think of Joseph. After being sold into slavery by his brothers, he rose to the position of steward over the household of one of Pharaoh's officials. When the master's wife tried to seduce him, he made his choice quickly and fled from the house (see Genesis 39:1–12). God's Word tells us to *run* from where we don't belong and to turn down all evil: "Flee the evil desires of youth and pursue righteousness, faith, love and peace" (2 Timothy 2:22); "reject every kind of evil" (1 Thessalonians 5:22). Quite literally, this is what Joseph found the strength to do. It's what we need the courage and strength to do today.

We tend to think people like Noah or Abraham, Joseph or Moses were somehow not like the rest of us. To us they appear to have been much more dedicated and determined. Yet all of them were ordinary! Do you know the one thing that distinguishes them? *They were willing to obey God.* That was their one common qualification, and God worked powerfully through each of them simply because they chose to stand for him.

Perhaps you don't think you have the strength to take a stand. The truth is, *none* of us does. None of us has this strength—in ourselves. What did Paul, who was seemingly fearless, say about the source of his strength?

It is God who makes both us and you stand firm. (2 Corinthians 1:21)

God has helped me to this very day; *so I stand here* and testify to small and great alike. (Paul speaking before King Agrippa and Governor Festus in Acts 26:22.)

If you're willing to be obedient to God, to act according to his will, to defend the truth of his Word, he will give you the strength!

God does not ask us to fight or win some great spiritual battle for him. He just asks us to turn to him for the strength to stand. He will win the battles; the ultimate victory is his. (If it were ours, we'd be tempted to take credit.)

God doesn't tell us to get into (or cause) a battle and then fight. He calls us to take a position and stand firm.

> Put on the full armor of God, so that you can *take your stand* . . . so that when the day of evil comes, you may *be able to stand* your ground, and after you have done everything, to *stand*. (Ephesians 6:11, 13)

> Do not be afraid or discouraged because of this vast army. For the battle is not yours, but God's. . . . You will not have to fight this battle. *Take up your positions; stand firm* . . . and the LORD will be with you. (2 Chronicles 20:15, 17)

We do not fight, and we're not the ones who secure the victory. We are to stand for God, his Word, his truth, his moral will.

Here's an illustration of what it means to stand for God. When soldiers in combat are ordered to take a stand, they're being told to secure and hold their position. They don't retreat, they don't give back a square inch of ground, they don't negotiate, and they don't surrender. They *stand*. This is what God asks us to do for him: Take a stand based on his Word, and then hold it. Don't retreat from it, don't negotiate it away, and don't surrender your convictions.

Others may mock you or slander you. But God says "stand."

It may cost you some friends. God says "stand."

It may cost you at work or at school. God says "stand."

It may affect your relationships with your family. God says "stand."

It will mean challenging the codes of the culture. God says "stand."

Truly loving God includes loving him with all our strength as we take an uncompromising stand for him and "contend for the faith" (Jude 3).

I Am to Love God With All My Soul

As to the final area in which God commands us to love him, what does it mean to love him with all your soul? This isn't the same as loving him with all your heart or mind. Your soul is what will survive death and live on into eternity,[7] and to love God this way, we begin by asking him to forgive our sins and come into our life. This is what we mean when we say someone has "become a Christian." He or she has accepted God's free gift of salvation.

Jesus Christ came for one overriding purpose: to die in your place and mine. He came to pay the price for our sin—death. God placed our sins on Jesus when he was on the cross: "God made him who *had no sin to be sin for us*, so that in him we might become the righteousness of God" (2 Corinthians 5:21). This means we don't have to be separated from him for all eternity. We can choose to live in his presence and experience the love, joy, peace, and deep-seated fulfillment he originally intended us to have. All we must do is accept his forgiveness by accepting Jesus' sacrifice on our behalf.

These verses explain this a bit more:

The wages of sin is death, but the *gift* of God is eternal life in Christ Jesus our Lord. (Romans 6:23)

222

God so loved the world that he gave his one and only Son, that whoever *believes* in him shall not perish but have eternal life. (John 3:16)

If you declare with your mouth, "Jesus is Lord," and *believe* in your heart that God raised him from the dead, you will be saved. (Romans 10:9)

Believe in the Lord Jesus, and you will be saved. (Acts 16:31)

If you've done this, you have chosen to love God with all your soul.

Now God wants you to be burdened for the souls of others who don't know Jesus. We all should be so burdened, for anyone lacking a saving relationship with him will endure eternal separation from God.

Perhaps you're not a Christian. Maybe you've never considered the unique truth claims of the Bible. Maybe you haven't understood who Christ is and why he came.

An incredible event took place in Jerusalem about two thousand years ago as Jesus hung on a Roman cross.

Jesus became our substitute. He took our place and he paid the penalty for our sins. This is what makes it possible for God to forgive us of all our sins. All we must do is accept his free gift of salvation.

If you've never accepted Jesus' offer and would like to do so, use this prayer as a guide, and ask him to come into your life and forgive your sins:

Dear God, I know I have sinned against you, and I know I need to be forgiven. I believe Jesus died on the cross for my sins, and I accept his free offer of forgiveness. Forgive my sins, Lord Jesus. Come into my life now as my Savior and Lord. Thank you for doing this for me. Thank you that I am now yours. Thank you that when my time here on earth is done, I will spend eternity in heaven with you. Amen.

If you have prayed this prayer from your heart, you have just become part of God's family. You've been restored to your Creator and will spend eternity with him.

Get a Bible and begin to read it. Try starting with the gospel of Matthew and read through the New Testament. Pray to God each day, thanking him for saving you and asking him to help you grow in your understanding of his Word. Ask him to help connect you with other believers and to help you find a church, a believing community, that teaches the Bible to help you mature in your faith.

So Why Are You a Christian?

Returning to where we started, why *are* you a Christian? Think about your response in light of all we've covered, and then write out your answer as best you can at this point. I am a Christian because . . .

.

In the days and years ahead, keep refining this statement. You will find that you add to it as you learn and grow.

Here's a response from each of us in answer to this question:

Norm Geisler: "I am a Christian because when I was a teenager, a holy God confronted me with my unholy life and informed me that his holy Son, Jesus, died for my sins and rose again from the dead (Romans 4:25) that I might have his holiness as a free gift of salvation (Romans 6:23).

"Without God's Holy Spirit convicting me of my unholy life (John 16:8), I would never have come to experience his holy love for me. Once I committed my life to him, he gave me the power to live a holy life. Before I trusted him as my Savior, I had an unholy and profane vocabulary. God miraculously took this from me and enabled me by his grace to praise him rather than curse him. Immediately, I wanted to know more about this God who transformed my life. I began by studying his Word and by discovering there was abundant support for believing that it is the Word of God.

"Now, sixty years later, I can say without reservation that I do not regret a moment of my life lived for him. I cannot too highly recommend it for you. Early on I adopted (and have kept) my life verse: 'For to me, to live is Christ and to die is gain' (Philippians 1:21). I added to this the motto: 'Only one life, 'twill soon be past, and only what's done for Christ will last.'"[8]

Patty Tunnicliffe: "I am a Christian because God has met all the needs of my heart—for love, forgiveness, restoration, hope, joy, and peace in times of greatest despair and in the darkest of nights. Also, because I am convinced by the evidence that Christianity is true to the exclusion of everything that contradicts it. Christianity provides the best answers to the questions of life; it's a perfect match for reality."

If you still struggle with your answer, continue to consider the evidence. Think about the claims of Jesus Christ and the evidence for his resurrection, about the Old and New Testaments being established as reliable documents you can trust. Then make it a priority to develop a better answer as you learn and grow. No Christian is exempt from giving an answer for the hope we have to anyone who may ask, and none is exempt from loving God with all their heart, soul, mind, and strength. Are you prepared to give an answer, and do you love him so fully that you'll serve him with all that you are?

Resources

Here are a few resources that deal with many of the questions we've asked.

John Ankerberg: *www.ankerberg.com/bio.htm*. A wide selection of resources on a wide variety of topics, designed to answer questions and help you grow in your understanding.

CANA: Christian Answers for the New Age, *www.christian answersforthenewage.org/*. An excellent source for articles and resources related to New Age topics and questions.

Ergun Caner: *www.erguncaner.com/*. Resources for anyone interested in learning how to understand Islam and converse with Muslims.

Norman Geisler: *www.normangeisler.net/*. Dr. Geisler's own site has a wide selection of apologetics articles and resources, and links to other helpful sites.

Alex McFarland, *Stand Strong in College*. Tyndale, 2008.

Illustra Media: *www.unlockingthemysteryoflife.com/*. Outstanding DVDs on DNA, creation, design.

International Legacy Institute: *www.internationallegacy.org/*. Home for several authors, their information, and books.

Lee Strobel: *www.leestrobel.com*. A variety of resources, speakers, videos.

Reasons for Belief: *www.reasons.org/*. This site will help with background and information related to creation and the design of the universe.

Ron Rhodes: *www.ronrhodes.org/*. Resources for Jehovah's Witnesses, Powerpoint presentations, prophecy.

Sandra Tanner: Utah Lighthouse Ministry, *www.utlm.org/*. The premier site for help with Mormonism.

Stand to Reason: *www.str.org/site/PageServer*. Mentoring, training in how to answer questions and defend your faith. Also podcasts, curricula, and other links.

The Truth Project—True U: *www.trueu.org/*. Excellent DVDs on the existence of God and the reliability of the Bible.

Books That Supplement What We Have Covered:

Norman Geisler:

The Big Book of Bible Difficulties: Clear and Concise Answers from Genesis to Revelation

From God to Us

I Don't Have Enough Faith to Be an Atheist

If God, Why Evil? A New Way to Think About the Question

Living Loud: Defending Your Faith

Making Sense of Bible Difficulties: Clear and Concise Answers from Genesis to Revelation

When Critics Ask: A Popular Handbook on Bible Difficulties

When Cultists Ask: A Popular Handbook on Cultic Misinterpretations

When Skeptics Ask: A Handbook on Christian Evidences

Who Made God? And Answers to Over 100 Other Tough Questions of Faith

Hugh Ross:
Beyond the Cosmos
The Creator and the Cosmos
The Fingerprint of God

Ron Rhodes:
5-Minute Apologetics for Today
What Does the Bible Say About . . . ? Easy-to-Understand Answers to the Tough Questions

Lee Strobel:
The Case for a Creator
The Case for Christ
The Case for the Real Jesus
The Case for Faith
The Case for the Resurrection
The Questions Christians Hope No One Will Ask

Notes

Chapter 3: God (Part I)

1. Thomas Jefferson, *The Jefferson Bible, or The Life and Morals of Jesus of Nazareth*, Kindle ed., 17:64, section 82, at 1021–1030.

2. Other views not discussed here (e.g., polytheism [many gods], or forms of finite godism [God is limited in power and/or perfection]) are less prevalent in today's West. See Geisler, *Christian Apologetics* (Baker, 2013).

3. J. Y. T. Greig, ed., *The Letters of David Hume* (Oxford: Clarendon, 1932), 1:187.

4. Quoted in Fred Hereen, *Show Me God: What the Message from Space Is Telling Us About God*, rev. ed. (Wheeling, IL: Day Star, 1997), 156.

5. Robert Jastrow, *God and the Astronomers*, 2nd ed. (Toronto: George J. McLeod, 1992), 14.

6. Hereen, *Show Me God*, 157.

7. Members of the American Scientific Affiliation, *Modern Science and Christian Faith*; Peter W. Stoner, "Astronomy and the First Chapter of Genesis" (Wheaton, IL: Van Kampen, 1948), 10.

Chapter 4: God (Part II)

1. Other kinds of cells, such as nerve cells, divide inside the body until they reach a certain level of maturity, and then they live until the person dies.

2. Stephen C. Meyer, "The Explanatory Power of Design: DNA and the Origin of Information" in William A. Dembski, ed., *Mere Creation* (Downers Grove, IL: InterVarsity, 1998), 244.

3. Ibid., 225.

4. Stephen W. Hawking, *A Brief History of Time* (New York: Bantam, 1988), 125.

5. Anthony Flew, *There Is a God* (New York: HarperOne, 2007), 117.

6. For a more detailed explanation, see Hugh Ross, *The Creator and the Cosmos* (Colorado Springs: NavPress, 1995, rev. ed.), 132.

7. Ibid., 134.

8. Ibid., 137–138.

9. Ross, *The Creator and the Cosmos,* 138.

10. Ibid., 135–136. Also see Hugh Ross, *The Fingerprint of God* (Orange, CA: Promise, 1991), 128–132 for an excellent discussion and a list of twenty different parameters that show how the earth has been fine-tuned to support life.

11. Hereen, *Show Me God*, 199, quoting Freeman Dyson, *Disturbing the Universe* (New York: Harper & Row, 1979), 250.

12. Norman L. Geisler, *Systematic Theology* (Minneapolis: Bethany House, 2002), 1.591.

13. C. S. Lewis, *Mere Christianity* (New York: Touchstone, 1943 [1996 ed.]), 21.

Chapter 5: Which God?

1. Environmental Literacy Council, "How Many Species Are There?" June 17, 2008. enviroliteracy.org/article.php/58.html. Accessed 07/19/2012.

2. John Ankerberg and John Weldon, *The Facts on Hinduism in America* (Eugene, OR: Harvest House, 1991), 32.

3. Ibid.

4. Ibid.

5. Mitch Pacwa, *Catholics and the New Age* (Ann Arbor, MI: Servant, 1992), 35.

Chapter 6: Miracles

1. CNN, "Flight 1549 crew: Hudson landing still on our minds," CNN.com/ US, February 11, 2009. cnn.com/2009/US/02/10/lkl.hudson.crew/index.html.

2. Norman L. Geisler, *Miracles and the Modern Mind: A Defense of Biblical Miracles* (Grand Rapids, MI: Baker, 1992), 145–154.

3. There is one two-stage miracle (Mark 8:22–26), illustrating the two stages of Israel's enlightenment with a blind man, but both stages involved an immediate intervention, and the whole event covered only a matter of minutes. But neither this nor any other miracle in the Bible was a gradual event.

4. For a solid discussion, see Norman L. Geisler and Abdul Saleeb, *Answering Islam: The Cross in the Light of the Crescent* (Grand Rapids, MI: Baker, 1993), 158–169.

5. C. S. Lewis, *Miracles* (New York: Macmillan, 1947, 1965), 169.

Chapter 7: The New Testament

1. Norman L. Geisler and William E. Nix, *A General Introduction to the Bible* (Chicago: Moody, 1968, rev. 1986), 213, quoting John A. T. Robinson, *Redating the New Testament* (Philadelphia: Westminster, 1976), 352.

2. Ibid., 213, quoting W. F. Albright, "Toward a More Conservative View" in *Christianity Today,* January 18, 1963, 3 (359).

3. See Richard Bauckham, *Jesus and the Eyewitnesses: The Gospels as Eyewitness Testimony* (Grand Rapids, MI: Eerdmans, 2006).

4. For a good discussion of this material, see: F. F. Bruce, *The New Testament Documents: Are They Reliable?* (Grand Rapids, MI: InterVarsity, 1943, reprint, 1992), 16; and Norman L. Geisler and Frank Turek, *I Don't Have Enough Faith to Be an Atheist* (Wheaton, IL; Crossway, 2004), 225.

5. Bart D. Ehrman, *Misquoting Jesus* (HarperCollins e-books), Kindle ed., at 199–206.

6. Geisler and Saleeb, *Answering Islam,* 233, quoting A. T. Robertson, *An Introduction to the Textual Criticism of the New Testament* (Nashville: Broadman, 1925), 22.

7. Norman Geisler and Ed Hindson, "Bible, Alleged Errors" in Ed Hindson and Ergun Caner, gen. eds., *The Popular Encyclopedia of Apologetics* (Eugene, OR: Harvest House, 2008), 100, quoting Philip Schaff, *Companion to the Greek NT and the English Version* (New York: Harper, 1883), 177.

8. Simon Greenleaf, *The Testimony of the Evangelists* (Grand Rapids, MI: Kregel, 1995), 31–32.

9. Ibid., 33.

10. Ibid., 47.

11. Greenleaf, *The Testimony of the Evangelists,* 35–36.

12. Ibid., 34–36.

13. Ibid.

14. See Norman L. Geisler, *Systematic Theology, Vol. 1,* chaps. 25–26.

15. F. F. Bruce, 101.

16. See, for instance, "Extra-biblical References to Jesus and Christianity," part of Historical and Archaeological Evidence for Christianity, at Rational Christianity-Christian Apologetics: rationalchristianity.net/jesus_extrabib.html. William Lane Craig, "Question 160, Subject: Thallus on the Darkness at Noon," at reasonablefaith.org.

See detailed explanation of this quote at tektonics.org/qt/thallcomp.html. All accessed 07/19/2012.

17. See F. F. Bruce, *Jesus and Christian Origins Outside the New Testament* (Grand Rapids, MI: Eerdmans, 1974).

18. See Norman Geisler and Joseph Holden, *The Popular Handbook of Archaeology and the Bible* (Eugene, OR: Harvest House, 2013).

19. Geisler and Nix, 195, quoting Nelson Glueck, *Rivers in the Desert: A History of the Negev* (New York: Farrar, Strauss & Cudahy, 1959), 31.

Chapter 8: Is Jesus God? (Part I)

1. "I *AM*" means God is self-existent and eternal, having no past, present, or future. He lives in eternity, so he simply *is*. He *is* I AM.

2. Leon Morris says: "This must have been a most unexpected move on [Jesus'] part. The soldiers had come out secretly to arrest a fleeing peasant. In the gloom they find themselves confronted by a commanding figure, who, so far from running away, comes out to meet them and speaks to them in the very language of deity." Leon Morris, *The Gospel According to John,* Ned B. Stonehouse, F. F. Bruce, and Gordon D. Fee, gen. eds., *The New International Commentary on the New Testament* (Grand Rapids, MI: Eerdmans, 1995, rev. ed.), 658.

3. See R. T. France, *The Gospel of Matthew* in Ned B. Stonehouse, F. F. Bruce, and Gordon D. Fee, gen. eds., *The New International Commentary on the New Testament* (Grand Rapids, MI: Eerdmans, 2007), 1029.

4. Lewis, *Mere Christianity,* 56.

5. Josh McDowell, *Evidence That Demands a Verdict,* rev. ed. (San Bernadino, CA: Here's Life, 1979), 111–112.

Chapter 9: Is Jesus God? (Part II)

1. "Iran hangs man who claimed to be God" report. January 31, 2011. iranian .com. See also torontosun.com/news/world/2011/01/31/17096306.html. Accessed 07/19/2012.

2. Hefner, Queen Elizabeth, Starr, and Graham at: Grassy Knoll Institute, January 2, 2010, "*50 Psychic Predictions for 2010,*" lotgk.wordpress.com/2010/01/02/50 -psychic-predictions-for-2010/.

3. "Nikki, Psychic to the Stars," Archived Predictions, 2010. psychicnikki.com/ predictions-archive.html#2010.

4. "*50 Psychic Predictions for 2010,*" Grassy Knoll Institute.

5. World Psychic, LaMont Hamilton, Predictions, 2010, part 1, worldpsychic .org/world-predictions/predictions-2010-part-i/.

6. Brad Ryan, "Psychic Experts Expect Mixed Bag in 2010," cairns.com.au, 12/31/09.

7. "*50 Psychic Predictions for 2010,*" Grassy Knoll Institute.

8. Ryan, "Psychic Experts Expect Mixed Bag in 2010."

9. B. A. Robinson, "46 failed end-of-the-world predictions that were to occur between 30 and 1920 CE, but didn't," Religious Tolerance.org, 06/14/2011, religious tolerance.org/end_wrl2.htm.

10. Ibid.

11. Ibid.

12. McDowell, 141–166. See also J. Barton Payne, *The Encyclopedia of Biblical Prophecy: The Complete Guide to Scriptural Predictions and Their Fulfillment* (New York: Harper & Row, 1973); Payne put the number at c. 100.

13. Harold W. Hoehner, *Chronological Aspects of the Life of Christ* (Grand Rapids, MI: Zondervan, 1978), Kindle edition, chap. 7, at 1668–1750, 1783.

14. Peter Stoner, *Science Speaks* (Online edition, rev. Nov. 2005, Don W. Stoner, 2002), sciencespeaks.net/ (locate at beginning of chap. 3). Accessed 07/19/2012.

15. Ibid.

16. Ibid.

17. Ibid. at end of chap. 3.

18. Marvin L. Bittinger, *The Faith Equation* (Literary Architects, 2007), chap. 4, 1867.

Chapter 10: Jesus' Resurrection

1. Geisler, *Miracles and the Modern Mind*, 29, quoting David Hume, *An Enquiry Concerning Human Understanding*, ed. C. W. Hendel (New York: Bobbs-Merrill, 1955), 10.1.122.

2. William D. Edwards, Wesley J. Gabel, Floyd E. Hosmer, "On the Physical Death of Jesus Christ," *JAMA* 255, no. 11 (03/21/86), 1455–63.

3. See Norman L. Geisler, *Christian Apologetics* (Grand Rapids, MI: Baker, 1976), 324. See also at F. F. Bruce, 113.

4. Geisler and Turek, 307. See page 430 for reference to Gary Habermas, *The Historical Jesus* (Joplin, MO: College Press, 1996), 218.

5. Josh McDowell Ministry, "Is there really solid evidence for the resurrection of Jesus Christ?" bethinking.org/resurrection-miracles/introductory/q-is-there-really-solid-evidence-for-the-resurrection-of-jesus-christ.htm. Accessed 07/19/2012. Quoting David Frederick Strauss, *The Life of Jesus for the People* (London: Williams and Norgate, 1879, 2nd ed.), vol. 1, 412.

6. See Hugh J. Schonfield, *The Passover Plot* (New York Disinformation Books, 2004, 40th anniversary edition).

7. Grant R. Jeffrey, *The Signature of God* (Colorado Springs: WaterBrook, 2010), Kindle ed., chap. 12, at 5252.

8. Ibid., at 5253.

9. See "Why Should I Believe in Christ's Resurrection?" at gotQuestions.org (2002–2012). gotquestions.org/why-believe-resurrection.html. Also, see Luckhoo's pamphlet "The Question Answered" at hawaiichristiansonline.com/sir_lionel.html (the final page contains this statement). Also see: John Ankerberg and John Weldon, *Ready With an Answer* (Eugene, OR: Harvest House, 1997), 25, quoting Sir Lionel Luckhoo, *What Is Your Verdict?* (Fellowship Press, 1984), 12, cited in Ross Clifford, *Leading Lawyers Look at the Resurrection* (Claremont, CA: Albatross, 1991), 112.

Chapter 11: Other Religious Books

1. Garry K. Brantley, "The Dead Sea Scrolls and Biblical Integrity," 1995. apologetics press.org/article/357. Accessed 07/19/2012.

2. Floyd Nolen Jones, *The Chronology of the Old Testament* (Humboldt, TN: KingsWord Press, 2002, 17th ed.), 11. christianmissionconnection.org/Which_Version_is_the_Bible.pdf. Accessed 07/19/2012.

3. Jeffrey L. Sheler, "Extraordinary Insights from Archaeology and History," *U. S. News and World Report,* "Is the Bible True?" 10/25/1999. positiveatheism .org/writ/isittrue.htm. Accessed 07/19/2006.

Chapter 12: Is Jesus the Only Way to God?

1. Richard Abanes, *Religions of the Stars: What Hollywood Believes and How It Affects You* (Minneapolis: Bethany House, 2009), Kindle ed., chap. 1, "Oprah's New Spirituality." From *The Oprah Winfrey Show,* January 3, 1994.

2. George Conger, "Presiding Bishop . . . 'Jesus is not the only way to God'" in *Church of England Newspaper,* 04/17/09. geoconger.wordpress.com/2009/04/17/presiding-bishop-jesus-is-not-the-only-way-to-god-cen-41709-p-7/ Accessed 07/19/2012.

3. Abanes, *Religions of the Stars,* chap. 1.

4. Lewis, *Mere Christianity,* 56.

Chapter 13: How Should the Truth Impact My Life?

1. For a list, see jewfaq.org/613.htm. Accessed 07/19/2012.

2. Frederick William Danker, ed., *A Greek-English Lexicon of the New Testament and Other Christian Literature,* rev. 3rd ed. (Chicago: University of Chicago Press, 2000), 508. Johannes P. Louw and Eugene A. Nida, eds., *Greek-English Lexicon of the New Testament, Based on Semantic Domains,* 2nd ed. (New York: United Bible Societies, 1989), 1.321. Spiros Zodhiates, *The Complete Word Study Dictionary: New Testament,* rev. (Chattanooga, TN: AMG, 1993), 819.

3. Louw and Nida, 324. Zodhiates, 436.

4. Danker, 484. Louw and Nida, 676, 700. Zodhiates, 787.

5. See Leviticus 11:44–45; 19:2; 20:7, 26; 1 Corinthians 1:2; Ephesians 1:4; Hebrews 12:14; 1 Peter 1:15–16.

6. Warren Baker and Eugene Carpenter, *The Complete Word Study Dictionary: Old Testament* (Chattanooga, TN: AMG, 2003), 976, 980.

7. Danker, 1098, Louw and Nida, 321, Zodhiates, 1494.

8. C. T. Studd, "Only One Life, 'Twill Soon Be Past."

Norman L. Geisler (PhD, Loyola University of Chicago) is distinguished professor of Apologetics and Theology at Veritas Evangelical Seminary in Murrieta, California. He is the author of some 80 books, including the *Baker Encyclopedia of Christian Apologetics*. He and his wife live in Charlotte, North Carolina. Learn more at www.normgeisler.com.

Patty Tunnicliffe (MA, Southern Evangelical Seminary) is a former public school teacher, Bible teacher, and conference speaker. She and her husband make their home in Santa Barbara, California.